The
Natic
Forest

CW00721663

By C.M. Dean

Cecilia lives in The National Forest
where she has been following the transformation
of the area with keen personal interest.
As an experienced globe-trotter, she decided to combine her love
for travel and exploration with her career expertise in information
technology, planning and management information.
The result is this guide for visitors, personally
researched and designed
by the author.

FOREWORD BY DAVID TAYLOR

"All who live within The National Forest will testify to the tremendous impact
it is already having on our lives. In only a decade, it has been a major factor in
the restoration of vast tranches of land despoiled by centuries of minerals
working, it is helping to rebuild the economy of our area and it provides
recreation and pleasure both for the villages and towns in its midst and for
growing numbers of visitors.

In this attractive and colourful guide, Cecilia Dean traces the geological
and historical roots of the forest, describes the many attractions of local
communities and illustrates it all with clear and helpful diagrams, maps, tables
and photographs.

It is an essential Forest guide for residents, tourists and students alike."

David Taylor, Member of Parliament – North West Leicestershire

The National Forest

In 1991 The National Forest was commissioned as the first new forest on this scale in England for over a millennium. As the word 'forest' conjures up a solid carpet of trees, it is easy to brush off the chances of this forest succeeding as impossible, especially as the region selected for the forest was once deeply scarred by coalmining, quarrying and earthworks.

The National Forest Company, established in 1995 to realise a vision of the Countryside Commission, took this challenge seriously and started:

> *to create, through working partnerships and with community participation, a*
> *new 200 square mile multi-purpose forest for the nation in the heart of England.*

- Mission statement of the National Forest Company

Early in 2003 a milestone towards this challenge was reached when the 5 millionth tree was planted near Alrewas beside the busy A38 motorway.

This book is an introduction to The National Forest: the history that shaped the past; the ongoing development of woodlands and parks; the places to visit and the activities to experience in the evolving Forest. All parks and venues are open all year round (except possibly Christmas Day and Easter Sunday for some venues) unless otherwise stated. Check for varying opening times. As the Forest concept is still being rolled out, detailed information on some activities and places of interest in the Forest are dynamic and may change. Contact addresses and reference information are therefore provided at convenient slots throughout the book.

The National Forest

Contents

The Decision

Why The National Forest? 4

History

Geological Landformation 6

Early Occupation 8

The Land Barons 10

Mining and Industries 12

20th Century Influence 14

The Future 15

The National Forest 17

1 Charnwood Forest 18

Heart of Charnwood Forest 20

Around the edge of the Forest 26

East of the Thringstone Fault 31

2 Coalfields 36

Medieval Coalfields 38

Coalville and Mining Villages 43

3 Coal and Clay 52

Around the Ashby Woulds 53

Further Afield 60

4 Parklands and Reservoirs 64

Ashby de la Zouch 66

Country Parks and Manors 70

Reservoirs 75

5 Rivers and Valleys 78

Burton upon Trent 80

The Trent Valley 84

6 Needwood Forest 90

Needwood 92

Activities 97

Towns and Villages 98

Historical Buildings and Ruins 100

Woodlands and Parks 102

Action Sport 104

Key Contacts

Councils 106

Tourist Information Centres 106

Environmental Trusts 107

Town/Village Websites 107

Travel 107

Accommodation 107

Activity Websites 107

Acknowledgements 108

Index 109

The Decision
Why The National Forest?

The National Forest is one of the most ambitious environmental projects to be undertaken in 1000 years of English history.

In 1987 the Countryside Commission pioneered the concept of a new forest for England and in 1991 set up a development team with Government backing. The objective of the team was to prepare a strategy and plan for this new forest, resulting in the establishment of the National Forest Company in 1995, specifically to create this contemporary forest in support of the country's future economic and environmental obligations.

It is this concept of both being contemporary and multi-purpose that makes The National Forest unique. It cuts across existing counties while at the same time moulding the towns and villages into a single forest, encouraging man to work and live in harmony with nature.

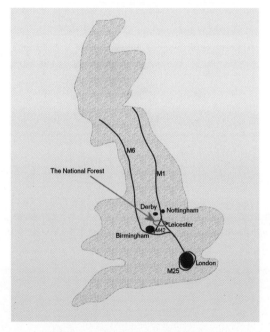

*The location of The National Forest
in the heart of England*

Developing a plan for a forest was already a major challenge, but deciding which part of England to transform, was not easy. Various locations were considered and in 1990 the choice fell on an area in the heart of England, stretching from the remainder of the ancient Needwood Forest west of Burton upon Trent in Staffordshire to the remainder of the ancient Charnwood Forest near Leicester in the east – an area which '...was once one of the least wooded parts of the country and was a region badly scarred by mining and mineral extraction'.

A journey through the ages corroborates the validity and wisdom of this choice.

Rejoining the old with the new:

New woodland planted next to the established Grace Dieu Wood in Thringstone (left)

Sence Valley Forest Park replacing a disused open cast mine (below)

History
Geological Landformation

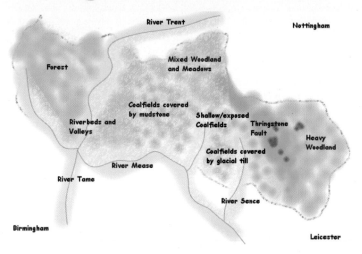

Geologically The National Forest can be divided into distinctly different land formations, namely river beds and valleys; lower parklands and meadows; clay and coal formations, and the Precambrian hills and rocky outcrops. Each has its own unique characteristics which influenced the history over the years.

The River Trent cuts through the western part of the forest and forms the southern border with its tributary, the Mease. Along the rivers the land lies below 75 m and the valleys, especially around the Trent, often flood onto the grassy floodplains, making it unsuitable for early settlers except in the areas of good drainage. The sandy grit in the river beds was found to be suitable for building material and roads and is still being extracted for this purpose in the Trent river valley.

Sloping up gently from the River Trent are the parklands and meadows of Melbourne and Needwood, as are those of the Mease and its tributaries such as the Sence around Heather, and the Gilwhiskaw brook from Measham towards Packington.

The most interesting of the land formations however can be found in the central and the eastern parts of The National Forest. The Midlands coal seams are found in a band from north west to the south eastern border of the region. In the northern section of the seam the coal measures of the Carboniferous period were shallow and exposed, while in the southern section the coal seams were overlaid by Mercia Mudstone and glacial till. This resulted in the northern shallow coal being mined since at least medieval times, while it only became possible to extract the concealed coal during the industrial revolution with the development of steam engines.

The coal fields of the region however have an abrupt boundary to the east formed by the Thringstone Fault. During the pre-historic volcanic period, eruptions caused the Palaeozoic rock in Charnwood to fold, creating the range of Warren hills and the Thringstone Fault stretching from Ticknall to Bardon. Although this terminated the coal seam, the rocks and limestone deposits have been quarried for centuries for road

building or, as in the case of the Swithland and Markfield quarries, for slate and building stone. The rocky conditions made the area unsuitable for cultivation and most parts remained covered in trees.

Ancient forest with a carpet of bluebells in spring

Rocky outcrops of Precumbrian Palaeozoic rock on top of Beacon Hill, clearly showing the tilt created by the folds

Early Occupation

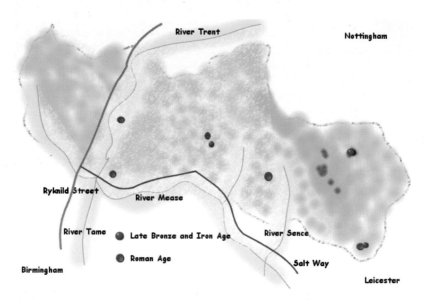

Unlike the southern parts of England, the Midlands around The National Forest showed limited signs of occupation before the Anglo-Saxons' arrival in the sixth century. Most of the area consisted of heavy woodland and was referred to as a wilderness in earlier publications and maps.

During the late bronze and iron age (1000 to 400 BC), hilltop forts were present on Beacon Hill and Budden Hill although the latter site has been destroyed by quarrying. Bronze and iron age implements were also found on other hills in the Warren Range, such as Bardon Hill and Croft Hill. Evidence of clearance for settlements onto the lower floodplains during the late Iron age (400 BC to 50 AD) was found at Woodhouse Eaves, Ratby and near Normanton le Heath.

Along the Trent and Tame the Tomsaetes tribe settled, later giving their name to Tamworth, south of The National Forest along the River Tame.

Even the Romans (70 to 410 AD) regarded this part of England as a thoroughfare between their main northern and southern strongholds, rather than a preferred settlement area. Ryknild Street, along the River Trent from the south through Derby to the north (now the A38), is the only major road through The National Forest dating back to Roman times. Two other Roman roads, Watling Street (now the A5) and Fosse Road touched the southern and eastern borders of the forest. Older than these routes, however, were the other ancient Salt Ways, linking the salt marches of Chester to the southern and

eastern parts of England. One such Salt Way branched off from the Ryknild (which also used to be a Salt Way) and ran along both sides of the Mease to the Eastern forests and Leicester, a major trading centre.

By the time of the Anglo-Saxon occupation, only a few villages and settlements were scattered across the area, mainly along the trading routes and river valleys. Evidence of Roman settlements were found at Ratby; near Alrewas; between Normanton le Heath and Ravenstone; and near Moira and Willesley, while names like Stretton en le Field imply the existence of a possible settlement next to a Roman Street.

The western part of The National Forest shows very little evidence of Roman occupation, or for that matter, any earlier occupation. The

Overlooking the edge of the bronze age hilltop fort on the top of Beacon Hill.

only settlements here were in the river valley of the Trent at areas of good drainage such as Barton-under-Needwood and Tatenhill.

Bronze age tool found on a site

Late Bronze Age axe head
- hollow to fit over the handle

The Land Barons

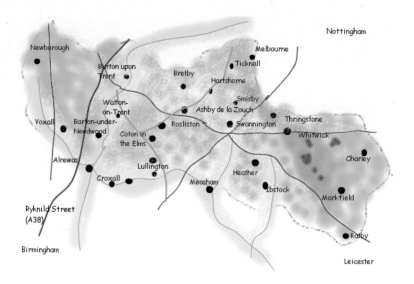

The main settlement of The National Forest area started during the era of the Anglo-Saxon and subsequent Danish occupation of the territory (fifth century onwards). Of the seven Kingdoms in England during this period, the Kingdom of Mercia was the most powerful by the second half of the eighth century and The National Forest lies in part of that Kingdom. It was during this period that the principle of thanes or landlords was introduced. Each lord had to provide the king with a number of trained warriors based on the amount of land owned. Evidence of this principle is seen in the history of places like Burton upon Trent and Barton-under-Needwood gifted by King Edmund to Wulfric Spot.

The Norman invasion in 1066 by William the Conqueror, however, heralded changes to this system with the introduction of the feudal system. Large areas of land (fiefs) were granted to chief nobles who subdivided it into smaller areas for lesser nobles and knights. By 1086 when William I commissioned the first census, the Domesday Book, to record the extent of his kingdom, the area covered by The National Forest was split roughly as follows:

- *Charnwood, the Melbourne parklands and Measham areas still belonged to the king.*
- *most of Needwood and the central region from Barton-under-Needwood to Staunton Hall was granted to Henry de Ferrers who was the Master of the Horse to William I at the battle of Hastings.*

Ashby Castle, originally built in the 12th century and fortified by lord William Hastings in the 15th century.

The remaining lands either belonged to monasteries, were smaller fiefdoms, or were already subdivided. Since the census of 1086 the land changed hands in many areas, but certain names remained prominent because of their influence on history — names like de Ferrers near Melbourne and most parts of The National Forest area, Hastings around the Ashby Woulds and Moira, Beaumont at Coleorton and Grace Dieu, and Grey at Groby and Bradgate Park, to name but a few. Needwood became part of the Duchy of Lancaster during the 14th century.

The legacy of the land barons and monasteries were the castles, stately homes and parks developed for and by them. Outside these parks, land was cleared for more efficient farming and more villages to house farm workers. Trees were needed to build and heat the houses — the reduction of forests started here.

This period also experienced the need for better roads such as the current A50 (A511) which possibly started as a 'feudal road'.

Staunton Harold Hall—first built in the 14th century and the home of the Shirley family (Earl of Ferrers) for centuries

Mining and Industries

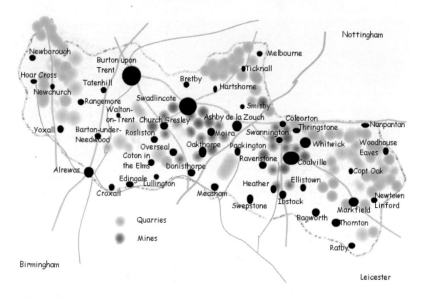

If deforestation of The National Forest area started with the feudal system, it accelerated during the mining and industrial revolution periods. The area became known for its rich natural resources under the Mercia mudstone and in the rocky outcrops, resulting in the exploitation of these deposits.

Coal was known to exist near the surface in the central regions of Coleorton and Swannington from as early as the 13th century, and retrieved through small opencast mines. So lucrative was this trade that at its peak there were up to 15 mines in this area and it became dangerous to walk around after dark except on the marked footpaths, from fear for falling into a mine. By the end of the 18th century a better quality shining coal (known as Leicester Bright) was discovered south of Whitwick underneath the glacial till that covered the mudstone. The recent invention of the steam engine made it feasible to sink deeper mines, and coal mining started in earnest in the Midlands. New towns like Coalville developed to house migrant miners and other towns and villages like Swadlincote, Whitwick, Ellistown and Ibstock grew to support the mines and secondary industries such as brickmaking. By 1889 28 mines were listed, 12 around Coalville to Lount and 16 between Donisthorpe and Swadlincote.

Ashby Woulds, in addition to coal, also showed deposits of iron ore nodules and a high quality clay. Both were mined and secondary industries developed such as iron foundries and potteries. More trees were needed to fuel the furnaces for these industries.

Moira Furnace, built by Sir Francis Hastings in 1804 and operational until 1812

Roman days until the closure of the quarry in the late 19th century. Quite a few of the smaller hills in the Warren hill range also disappeared because of the quarrying. The quarry near Melbourne rendered limestone, baked in kilns for building material. The sand and gravel in the Trent basin was extracted for road building.

Along the eastern side of the Thringstone Fault, there was no coal, but the Precambrian rock was, and still is being quarried for building material and roadworks. One of the best known quarries was the Swithland Quarry in Charnwood. It was known for the high quality blue slate, which was mined since the

The result of the industrialisation is the near total destruction of the woodland in the region. Not only were the forests destroyed for fuelling of machinery, but the woodland was replaced by mine dumps and spoil heaps.

Snibston No 2 Colliery in Coalville, sunk in the 1830s and now converted into a discovery theme park on mining and related industries.

20th Century Influence

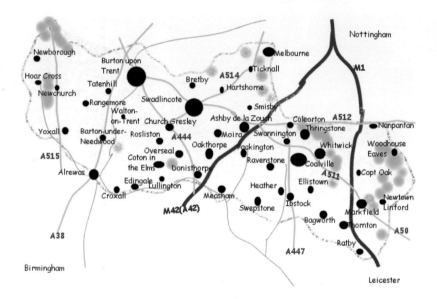

By the middle to the end of the 20th century the coal mines were becoming uneconomical and closed down one by one. Most of the coal mines operational in the region by the end of the 19th century were closed by the 1980s and the region had to regenerate itself or go into a fatal decline.

By this time a comprehensive set of roads were in place: the M1 was passing through the eastern part of the region and the M42/A42 linked the M1 to the M6 and Birmingham just south of Ashby de la Zouch. Most of the railway system, built by the Robert Stephenson in the 1830s to service the mines, closed down as part of the Beeching reforms in the 1960s, but the main lines still run through Burton upon Trent and to the east along the Midlands line.

The M1 and A42 encouraged the development of light industry, small service businesses and large warehousing in towns like Coalville (Bardon Industrial Estate), Burton upon Trent and Ashby de la Zouch, with other towns and villages setting up business centres to meet the need for diversification. Small villages became popular as commuter residential areas for the larger cities surrounding the area, such as Birmingham, Leicester, Derby and Nottingham.

The forests of Charnwood and Needwood were however reduced to small patches and although County/District Councils and Nature Trusts started to regenerate disused mines and quarries from the middle of the 20th century, The National Forest decision came as a welcome boost.

The Future

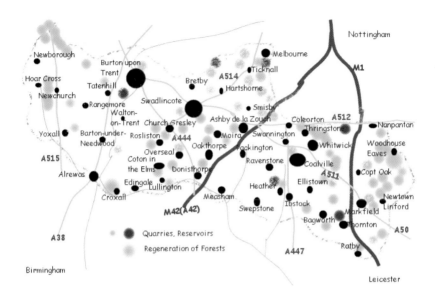

Whereas regeneration of disused mines and quarries received some attention towards the end of the 20th century, it was the vigour and leadership of the National Forest Company that really set the ball rolling during the last five years of the century. In the Company's 2001 Annual Report, and on their website, they summarised their objectives and progress as follows:

First and foremost it is the job of the National Forest Company to achieve the implementation of The National Forest Strategy – the great Forest vision which was taken to full public consultation and won nationwide acclaim. The aim for the area, as set out in the Forest Strategy, is to create a new 200 square mile, truly contemporary, multi-purpose forest, which, over time, will support the country's future economic and environmental needs through:

- *Creating a diverse landscape and wildlife habitat and enhancing biodiversity*
- *Providing alternative productive uses for agricultural land*
- *Increasing public access to, and awareness of, the countryside*
- *Creating new resources for education, sport, recreation and tourism*
- *Stimulating economic enterprise and creating employment opportunities*
- *Contributing to the UK's homegrown sustainable timber supplies.*

By 2002 the wooded cover had more than doubled from 6% ten years ago to 14% (6700 ha), well on track towards the long term goal of 30% cover. The 5 millionth tree was planted in early 2003. In the words of Susan Bell, the chief executive of the National Forest Company:

> The experience learnt over the six years of the Forest's implement-ation should prove invaluable as a model for the wider countryside. The integration of land use, environmental enhancement and economic regeneration is a successful formula, whether that land use is based on agriculture, mineral extraction, natural habitat or woodland. A willingness by farmers, landowners and a whole host of other partners, to part-icipate in this great venture bears testament to that success.

The methodical regeneration of the disused sites into woodland and water parks is giving us back the forests lost over the centuries. Come and experience the diversity of ancient forests adjacent to the excitement of new forests in the making. Come and experience The National Forest.

Regeneration

Growing the new Bagworth Heath Forest on the site of the disused mine

The National Forest

The aim of the National Forest Company is to mould the designated areas in the heart of England into a 'contemporary, multi-purpose forest to support the country's economic and environmental needs'. This exciting project offers a balance between the restoration of environmental damage inflicted on the countryside by mining, extractions and the industrial revolution, and the sensitive support and enhancement of tomorrow's industries such as tourism, light industries and mixed farming.

The geological makeup of the area, and man's exploitation of the natural resources, divide The National Forest into six essentially different sectors, each with its unique history, problems and solutions. The Forest map has therefore been divided into the sectors as indicated on the map below.

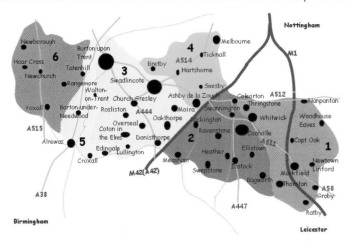

Sectors covered in The National Forest

1. Charnwood Forest   18
2. Coalfields   38
3. Coal and Clay   53
4. Parkland and Reservoirs   66
5. Rivers and Valleys   80
6. Needwood Forest   92

Each sector will start with references to Information Centres and relevant websites for more detail, and interesting places to visit in the area. The sector is then further subdivided into easily achievable 'day-trips' for the whole family, allowing details of towns, villages, places of interest and activities to be presented in a format to help you plan and enjoy your visit.

1 Charnwood Forest

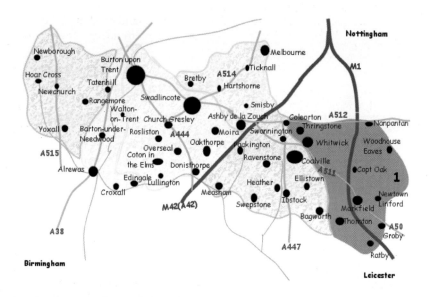

EXPLORE CHARNWOOD FOREST IN THREE SECTIONS

- Heart of Charnwood Forest (Newtown Linford to Nanpantan)
- Around the edge of the Forest (Blackbrook Reservoir to Ratby)
- East of the Thringstone Fault (Thringstone to Thornton Reservoir)

Charnwood's distinctive character was sculptured by the underlying pre-Cambrian rock formation. Pre-historic volcanic eruptions and folding of the Palaeozoic rock formed what is today referred to as the Thringstone Fault. The fault stretches from Ticknall in the north of The National Forest to south of Bardon Hill, clearly ending the coalfields to the west of Charnwood Forest with a range of hills and rocky outcrops. Two of the most prominent of these hills are Bardon Hill (278m/912ft) and Beacon Hill (250m/820ft) and, being the highest points in Leicestershire, they offer excellent views over the countryside. Relics from early bronze age hill fort occupation were found on Beacon Hill.

The absence of coal shielded Charnwood from the fate of mining that devastated the central part of The National Forest. However, it did not escape altogether as the underlying rock has been, and is still being quarried.

Swithland Quarry, towards the east of the forest, was quarried for its well-known and popular blue slate from Roman times up to the late 19th century, as evidenced by the roof slates of many of the surrounding houses.

Active quarries can still be found near Whitwick, Bardon and Stanton under Bardon, although effort is being made to conceal the earthworks by planting tree shelters around the quarries.

Most of Charnwood Forest was designated parkland over the centuries and therefore left undeveloped. As a result it contains ancient forests and parks which are very popular with the public. It offers excellent walks, rides and birdwatching facilities in the parks, and fishing in the reservoirs.

Information in Brief

Information Centres:

Leicestershire County Council,
Tourism Section
County Hall, Glenfield, Leics LE3 8RJ
Tel: 0116 265 7039
e-mail: tourism@leicestershire.gov.uk
Website: www.leics.gov.uk

Coalville Tourist Information Centre
Snibston Discovery Park, Ashby
Road, Coalville LE67 3LN
Tel: 01530 813608
e-mail:
coalville.tic@nwleicestershire.gov.uk
Website: www.nwleics.gov.uk

Loughborough Tourist
Information Centre
Town Hall, Market Place,
Loughborough LE11 3EB
Tel: 01509 218113
Website: www.charnwoodbc.gov.uk

Woodlands and Parks:

Charley: Cathill and Burroughs
Woods
Markfield: Altar Stones
Nanpantan: Outwoods and Jubilee
Wood
Newtown Linford: Bradgate Park
Ratby: Martinshaw Wood, Pear Tree
Woods and Ratby Burroughs
Swithland: Swithland Park
Stanton under Bardon: Billa Barra

Thringstone: Grace Dieu Wood
Whitwick: Cademan Wood
Woodhouse Eaves: Beacon Hill
Country Park, Broombriggs Farm,
Felicity's Wood and Martin's Wood

Lakes and Reservoirs:

Blackbrook Reservoir (walks)
Cropston Reservoir (fishing)
Groby Pool (picnics)
Nanpantan Reservoir (fishing)
Swithland disused quarries (club
diving)
Thornton Reservoir (fishing)

Places of Interest:

Copt Oak: Bardon Hill, Ulverscroft
Groby Old Hall
Priory ruins
Nanpantan: Home Farm
Newtown Linford: Bradgate Park
and Bradgate House
Thringstone: Grace Dieu Priory ruins
Whitwick: Mount St Bernard Abbey

Relevant Websites:

www.go-fish.co.uk
www.birdinguk.co.uk
www.luec.freeserve.co.uk
(Underwater exploration club)
www.pcuk.org
(Pony club)
www.leicesterclimbs.f9.co.uk
www.nationalforest.org

Heart of Charnwood Forest

Charnwood Forest is one of the oldest surviving forests in The National Forest. Volcanic folding of the rock formation during pre-historic periods, gave it an upland forest character so that it remained sparsely occupied. Only a few small villages can be found in the forest with the larger developments at the edges.

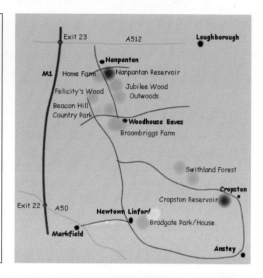

Directions

- Exit the M1 at junction 23 east towards Loughborough
- Turn right into Snell's Nook Lane (just before the two garages)
- Cross the traffic lights in Nanpantan. The **Nanpantan Reservoir** will be on the left and **Home Farm** entrance on the right just outside Nanpantan
- **Jubilee Wood and Outwoods** are next on the left and the lower car park for **Beacon Hill Country Park** is on the right
- At the T-junction turn left for a detour visit to **Woodhouse Eaves**, or
- Turn right. **Broombriggs Farm trail** parking is on the left. Further on top of the hill is the **Beacon Hill** upper car park to the right
- At the next crossing turn right for a detour visit to Beacon Cottage Farm with **Felicity's Wood and Martin's Wood, else**
- Turn left towards Cropston. The car park for **Swithland Wood** is on the left after approximately 5 km (2.2 miles)
- The **Cropston Reservoir** is on the right just before reaching Cropston village
- In Cropston take the first road right towards Anstey and from there the road towards **Newtown Linford**
- The main car park for **Bradgate Park** and **Bradgate House** is in the village of Newtown Linford
- The road from Newtown Linford towards Markfield will take you on to the A50 and then back to the M1 at junction 22.

NANPANTAN RESERVOIR

Nanpantan Reservoir is a 2 ha (5 acre) man-made lake just outside Nanpantan, managed by Severn Trent Water. It offers easy access for anglers by means of a pathway all around the lake. Permits are essential and each angler may be accompanied by one non-fishing guest. The reservoir is known for carp, bream and plenty of small perch and roach.

Fishing at Nanpantan Reservoir

HOME FARM

Home Farm in Woodhouse Lane, Nanpantan, is an organic farm with play area, barn and Victorian garden and ample parking space. The farm has a traditional Forest farm café, restaurant and shop selling unusual ethical crafts.

There are clearly marked walks taking you through Puzzle Wood to a picnic area at the top of Little Buck Hill. This walk also joins up with Jubilee and Outwood trails. Parking for the walks are in lay-bys in Woodhouse Eaves Lane and Deans Lane.

OUTWOODS AND JUBILEE WOOD

These woods, south of Nanpantan, were once part of the Charnwood Hunting park where young deer were put out when ready for hunting. Jubilee Wood is a 10 ha (25 acre) mixed woodland, presented to Leicestershire County Council in 1977 to commemorate the Queen's Silver Jubilee.

The Outwoods is a 40 ha (100 acre) typical old woodland, situated on a ridge overlooking Loughborough and is home to a rich collection of plants, animals and birds. It is a site of special scientific interest and in spring time the ground is covered with a carpet of bluebells. Car parking and toilet facilities are available at the woods and there are clearly marked walking trails.

WOODHOUSE EAVES

Woodhouse Eaves is a picturesque working village with many stone cottages roofed with blue Swithland slate. It takes its name from the location on the high edges (eaves) of Charnwood Forest. The village wraps around Windmill Hill, the site of a 19th-century post windmill. The base of the old windmill is still there.

Bluebells in Spring

BROOMBRIGGS FARM

The 55 ha (136 acres) mixed arable and stock farm near Woodhouse Eaves, was presented to Leicestershire County Council in 1970. The farm applies modern farm practice and countryside management techniques.

Broombriggs offers a 2.4 km (1.5 mile) well marked, farm trail with information boards explaining the working of the farm. The trail is popular with hikers and horse riders all year round, but the information boards are only displayed during the summer months.

Broombriggs Farm Trail

BEACON HILL

At 250 m (820 ft), Beacon Hill is the second highest point in Leicestershire with a totoscope and good views from the top. On a clear day you should be able to see the spire of Lincoln Cathedral in the distance! The splintery volcanic rocky outcrops on the top are some of the oldest in England, estimated to be 700m years old.

A scheduled ancient monument of a late bronze age hill fort settlement (4000 – 1000 BC) can be found on the hill in the form of ditches between the stone wall and the upper car park. Pottery and later bronze age artefacts have been found, including a mould for axe heads, together with signs of occupation during the early iron age (600 BC to 43 AD).

The name of the hill possibly refers to a fire which was lit on the hill as warning of the approaching Spanish Armada during the reign of Queen Elizabeth I in 1588.

Beacon Hill Country Park covers 100 Ha (250 acres) of mixed woodland, heathland, grassland and adjoining farmland. It has two car parks – near the bottom and top of the hill, with toilets, picnic places, disabled and baby-changing facilities. Bio-degradable benches from piled silver birch trunks have been placed conveniently around the park.

West Beacon Field near the lower car park, contains over 8,000 newly planted indigenous trees and shrubs, representing all 28 species of trees native to the UK. Popular activities in the park include walking, dogwalking, kite flying from the top of the hill, bird-watching and horse riding. Riding and walking trails are clearly marked.

Totoscope and view from Beacon Hill

Two further Woodland Trust developments can be found on the nearby Beacon Cottage farm. Felicity's wood is a 9 ha (22 acre) mixed development and Martin's Wood a 5 ha (12 acre) newly planted broadleaved development. Both sites offer good views, information boards and limited parking.

SWITHLAND AND SWITHLAND WOODS

Swithland is a pleasant residential village on the edge of Charnwood Forest, but it is the wood that is better known in The National Forest. Swithland Park is 56 ha (140 acre) of woodland containing remnants of original Charnwood Forest oak, birch, alder and lime trees. It has Ancient Woodland status with a rich collection of birds, insects and plants. A good network of paths makes it suitable for walkers, cyclists and horse riders. Birdwatchers should watch out for lesser spotted woodpeckers, wood warblers and woodcocks.

Interesting in Swithland Park are the two disused and water filled quarries, once famous for the dark blue slate quarried there from Roman times up to the late 19th century. Some houses in neighbouring villages such as Newtown Linford, Swithland and Woodhouse Eaves still have the Swithland slate roofs, while blue slate headstones can be seen in the graveyards.

Swithland blue slate and the quarry

Today the water filled disused quarries have been fenced off and are frequented by local clubs for diving and climbing. The southern quarry is approximately 50m (164ft) deep and is specifically used for practising deep, cold water diving (not for the inexperienced).

CROPSTON RESERVOIR

East of Bradgate Park is the Cropston Reservoir, opened in 1870 and into which the river Lin flows. This reservoir is under management of Severn Trent Water and is also a popular venue for birdwatching and fishing. There are good visitor centre and conference facilities at the site.

Fishing at Cropston Reservoir

NEWTOWN LINFORD

Newtown Linford is a typical forest village, off the B5327, with thatched or slate-roofed cottages and timbered style buildings built along winding streets. It features a cricket field (behind the church) which has been acknowledged as one of the most attractive village fields in the country.

The most accepted meaning of the village name is 'the new town by the ford over the river Lin', which flows through the town. The ford used to be at the junction of Markfield Lane and Main Street, but it has to be said that the 'new' town dates back to the 13th century! The southern and main car park and entrance to Bradgate Park is in Newtown Linford. Lane End Farm near the village is a farm shop selling animal feeds, fresh produce and fruit juices, cakes and preserves. It offers facilities for the disabled.

BRADGATE PARK

Bradgate park is the most visited park in Leicestershire. It covers 344 ha (850 acres) of hilly countryside and woodland, with outcrops of volcanic granite. Bradgate's owners can be traced to the de Ferrers family of Groby in the 12th century, and much of the land was used for hunting and has therefore never been farmed. The small village of Bradgate was cleared by the Grey family in the 14th century to enlarge the park.

The park was sold by the Grey family to Charles Bennion of Thurnby in 1926 and in 1928 he gave it to Leicestershire County as a place for public enjoyment. The park contains red and fallow deer and the river Lin forms weirs and ponds for families to picnic. It is popular for walking, horse riding, cycling and in winter, sledging. Its wide variety of animals and birds also makes it a popular venue for birdwatching.

On top of the hill is a tower (folly) believed to have been built in 1784 for a retainer of the 5th Earl of Stamford who was killed accidentally on the spot. This folly, called Old John, is a well known landmark in Leicestershire.

Silhouette of Old John against the Bradgate skyline.

View from the top of Bradgate Park with rocky outcrops.

Three car parks provide entrance to different parts of the park. The western entrance is closest to the summit and Old John folly. The south eastern entrance is near Cropston Reservoir and the southern entrance in Newtown Linford leads to the Bradgate House ruins and information centre.

BRADGATE HOUSE

Bradgate House was built between 1490 and 1500 by Sir Thomas Grey (the 1st Marquis of Dorset, and son of Elizabeth Woodville) as one of the first luxury country houses after the era of castles. The house was occupied until around 1750, but today only the chapel is still intact and is used as a museum, which is open from March to November.

One of the most famous occupants of Bradgate House was Lady Jane Grey, the granddaughter of Henry VII who was born (1537) and spent most of her childhood days there. She married her cousin

Edward VI, the son of Henry VIII and Jane Seymour. After his death in 1553 she became queen of England for nine days before she was deposed and subsequently beheaded by order of Mary Tudor.

On a dark St Sylvester's night (31st December) you may still see a coach with four horses driving through Bradgate park towards the house carrying Lady Jane Grey with her head on her lap!

Lady Jane Grey, the "Queen for nine days" was born, and spent her childhood years in Bradgate House

Above: A fallow deer in Bradgate Park
Below: Bradgate House

Around the Edge of the Forest

Around the edges, the woodland of Charnwood Forest give way to open farmland and the larger villages of Markfield and Groby. Over the centuries it was easier to clear the edges of the forest for development as these villages; the ruins of Ulverscroft Abbey; and Mount Saint Bernard Abbey bear witness to.

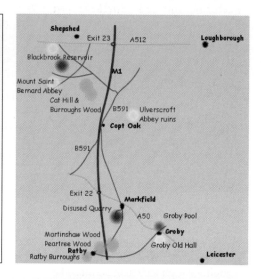

Directions

- Exit M1 at junction 23 west on the A512 towards Ashby de la Zouch
- Cross two traffic lights and turn left in to Charley Road towards Oaks in Charnwood. The road passes the **Fenney Windmill** on the right and a public footpath to **Blackbrook Reservoir** (right) at Botany Bay
- At the next crossroad follow the signs towards **Mount Saint Bernard Abbey**
- Returning from the Abbey, pass through Charley and the footpath to **Cat Hill and Burroughs Woods**, on to **Copt Oak** on the B591.
- Park at Copt Oak pub to explore the hamlet and hike to **Ulverscroft Abbey**, a 5 km (2 mile) return walk
- At Copt Oak follow the road to **Markfield**, cross the A50 and stay on Hill Lane to **Markfield Quarry** on the left or turn right for **Altar Stones** and **Blacksmith's Fields**
- To reach **Ratby**, it will be easiest to return to the A50 towards Leicester and turn off through **Groby Village** towards **Ratby**, **Martinshaw Wood** and **Peartree Wood**
- Rejoin the M1 again at junction 22 or 21 from Ratby.

Fenney Windmill is a landmark visible from the A512. It is a listed building on the outskirts of Shepshed, on the border of The National Forest, and is privately owned.

Fenney Windmill viewed from the A512

BLACKBROOK RESERVOIR

Blackbrook Reservoir was built in the 1790s to feed the newly constructed Charnwood Forest Canal from Loughborough to Thringstone. The canal was built to transport coal from the Swannington/Coleorton pits to Loughborough and the Leicester Market. After a heavy snowstorm in 1799 the reservoir and canal walls collapsed and flooded the surrounding villages. The canal was never rebuilt, but a new reservoir was constructed in 1907.

The reservoir is owned by Severn Trent Water and apart from open access footpaths, is not open to the public.

The Cat Hill and Burroughs Woods at Charley between the Blackbrook Reservoir and Copt Oak are often included in the hikes around Blackbrook Reservoir.

MOUNT ST BERNARD ABBEY

Unlike the local medieval priory ruins such as Grace Dieu and Ulverscroft, Mount St Bernard Abbey, east of Whitwick, was founded as recently as 1835. It has the unique distinction of being the first Catholic Abbey built in the country since the Reformation and the only Cistercian Monastery in England. The Abbey was built with local stone and was not finally finished until 1939. The ceremony of Consecration was only held after the second world war in 1945.

From 1856 to 1881 the Monastery became the largest Reformatory in the country for Catholic juvenile delinquent boys, housing up to 250 boys. Today it is a working monastery and open to the public as a retreat. It has a large working pottery as well as carpentry and printing shops and offers a shop and public conveniences for casual visitors.

Mount Saint Bernard Abbey is the first Catholic Abbey to be built in England since the Reformation

Mount Saint Bernard Abbey with Calvary Hill in the background

COPT OAK

The name Copt Oak is rumoured to be derived from a 2000 year old pollarded oak tree which stood in the corner of the churchyard until 1855. It was thought to have been used as a meeting place for the forest swanimotes during medieval times, and as a rallying point during the Civil War. A swanimote according to Brewer's Dictionary of Phrase and Fable is:

Typical building style: brick corners, rock wall, slate roof

> A court held thrice a year before forest verderers by the stewart of the court. So called because the swans or swains (freeholders, herdsmen, shepherds or youths), were the jurymen. This court was incident to a forest.

The hamlet was only developed after the enclosure act during the early 19th century and grew around the tree. A new oak tree was planted again in the churchyard in 1996 and copted in 2000 to commemorate the historic tree.

Oak tree copted in 2000

Today most of the buildings in Copt Oak are listed for their typical local style of stone walls and brick corners. The old school house was converted into a Youth Hostel until its recent sale to private owners. Popular hiking routes originate from Copt Oak to the top of Bardon Hill, Mount St Bernard Abbey, and the Ulverscroft Priory ruins.

ULVERSCROFT PRIORY RUINS

Ulverscroft is an agricultural parish in the Charnwood Forest without a specific village.

Ulverscroft Priory was founded in the 11th century by Robert de Bossu as a small refuge for Augustinian Eremites. A nearby small priory, Charley, was founded by Robert's son, but united with Ulverscroft around 1465. The Priory kept open house for wayfarers and supported the poor and needy in surrounding villages.

Ulverscroft Priory ruins

The legend of Agnes Litherland is linked to the priory. Agnes was promised in marriage to William de Mavesyn, a knight from Northumberland, but met and married Don Giraidi Sforza in secret in Cadiz, Spain, while on a holiday shortly before her planned wedding. Sforza was a violent man, and when Agnes thought he was killed by lightning in Cadiz, she came back to England and became an inmate of Ulverscroft Priory. William traced her to the priory and they planned to run away, but Sforza who survived the lightning strike, killed William and tried to kill Agnes as well. After this Agnes became the last prioress of Grace Dieu Priory near Thringstone, where a further scandal was linked to her name.

Today the semi-ruined remains of the Ulverscroft Priory are on private land and can only be reached via a footpath from Copt Oak over Whitcroft Lane, or from Priory Lane. Car parking is available at Copt Oak and a good hiking map is advisable.

Disused Markfield Quarry

ancient local crayfish, uncontaminated by imported species. Diving is therefore strictly controlled to prevent contamination. Other nearby popular spots for walking and picnics are Altar Stones, a 2 ha (5 acre) heathland with rocky outcrops of geological interest, and Blacksmith's Field, a Woodland Trust development.

Climbing the Altar Stones

MARKFIELD

Markfield is one of the highest villages in Leicestershire and also one of the coldest. It is a thriving village next to the A50, within easy commuting reach from Leicester and Coalville's Industrial Centres. The village has an active equestrian centre and pony club.

The Markfield Quarry extracted syenite for buildings, curbstones and road building during the mid 19th century. It was called 'Hill Hole' locally but was discontinued when it filled with water. Due to its remote location, the water is said to contain

GROBY

The names of Groby and Ratby indicate a Danish origin (-by for town or settlement), dating them to at least the ninth century. The villages were part of property gifted to Hugh de Grandmesnil after the 1066 Norman Conquest, but soon changed hands when his son pawned them to Robert Beaumont, the Earl of Leicester. The Beaumonts owned the land until around 1300, when the de Ferrers family took over, and in 1440 it passed to the Greys through marriage of Sir Edward Grey.

Groby Old Hall, the house of the Greys until Thomas Grey built Bradgate House in 1490, is still in the village. The Grey family had an interesting history. Sir Edward's son, Sir John, married Elizabeth Woodville in 1457. The Greys were however supporting the losing side in the War of the Roses and Sir John was killed in the Battle of St Albans in 1461. When King Edward IV became king, the Greys lost their property, but had it restored to them when Elizabeth married the king in 1464. Her grand-daughter, Lady Jane Grey born in Bradgate House, was later to become the 'Nine-day Queen'.

Today Groby is a thriving village with its own light industry and as a commuter village for Leicester. Granite quarries around the village used to, and still provide building material for buildings and roads. Groby Pool is a popular spot for picnics.

Groby Pool

RATBY

Ratby is one of the few places in The National Forest where remnants of an early iron age settlement were found. A ditch in Ratby Burroughs is proof of this iron age and possibly later Roman settlements. Leicester used to be the regional capital for the Midlands during the Roman days with the name of Ratae Corieltauvorum. It is thought that Ratby used to be called Ratae from this period. Aerial photography also shows traces of Saxon buildings near Rothley Brook and according to a local legend the Devil used to throw timbers from the local Saxon church into this brook. Nothing is left of the church today.

Worth a visit are the Woodland Trust forests near the village. Martinshaw Wood covers 140 Ha (347 acres) of woodland, offering a variety of paths, including a 2 km (1.24 miles) all-abilities circular trail through a mixture of mature and ancient oak woods, mixed conifers and broadleaved woodlands. During the 1940s Martinshaw wood was a managed plantation of conifers, which is now being managed back to the original broadleaf trees by the Trust. The Trust area also contains newly planted native trees in the adjacent Pear Tree wood.

Martinshaw Wood all-abilities trail

East of the Thringstone Fault

Situated at the edge of the Charnwood Forest and Warren Hill range, this area is rich in established and newly planted woodlands and rocky outcrops. The rocks form part of the Precambrian granite or syenite and is still quarried for road gravel.

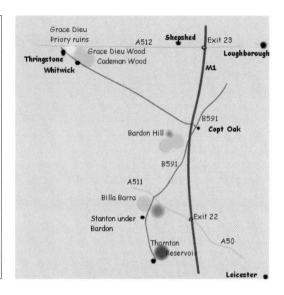

Directions

- Exit the M1 at junction 23 and turn west on the A512 towards Ashby de la Zouch to the Thringstone turnoff. The A512 passes the **Grace Dieu Priory ruins** to the left near the turnoff
- Park at the Bull's Head at the Thringstone turnoff for a footpath from the car park towards the ruins and through **Grace Dieu Wood** (also **Cademan Wood)**
- Drive through **Thringstone** and **Whitwick**. The **Hermitage Leisure** centre is to the right in Silver Street
- Outside Whitwick pass the Whitwick quarry on the left and on to a T junction with the B591 at Copt Oak. Park at Copt Oak for a hike to the top of **Bardon Hill** (about 5 km, 2 mile return)
- Continue with the B591 to the roundabout where it crosses the A511
- Cross the A511 towards **Stanton under Bardon. The Billa Barra reserve** is on the right with views to the Cliffe Hill disused quarry from the top of the hill, to the south east
- Follow the signs south to Thornton and **Thornton Reservoir**
- Retrace steps to the A511 and rejoin the M1 at junction 22.

GRACE DIEU AND THRINGSTONE

Grace Dieu priory, visible from the A512 just before the turnoff into Thringstone, was founded by Lady Roesia de Verdun to house Augustinian nuns around 1235. It was one of only two medieval nunneries in Leicestershire and is a nationally significant Scheduled Ancient Monument. Like most nunneries it was relatively poor but offered a spiritual sanctuary, shelter for travellers, and education for girls.

Statue of a nun overlooking the Grace Dieu Priory ruins

Grace Dieu Priory ruins

A scandal surrounded the priory when 'irregularities' were rumoured of a nursery being run by the priory, led by the Prioress, Agnes Litherland herself. Can the ghostly sightings of the 'White Lady' at nearby bus stops and close to the priory be linked to the disgraced Prioress?

The Order was suppressed and dissolved in 1539 by Henry VIII after which the Priory became a private residence of John Beaumont for 150 years. Francis Beaumont (1584 to 1616), the famous Elizabethan dramatist and poet, was born and lived here. He wrote many poems and plays in collaboration with John Fletcher, of which *'The Knight of the Burning Pestle'* and *'The Maid's Tragedy'* are but two examples still read and studied today. He was buried in Westminster Abbey in 1616. The Priory ruins are today in the grounds of the Grace Dieu Manor School and have recently been awarded lottery money to be stabelised and eventually opened as a tourist attraction.

Grace Dieu Manor and Thringstone have a further claim to fame in their association with the Rt Hon Charles Booth PC (1840 – 1916), the great philanthropist and pioneer of social research, whose tomb and epitaph can be found on the north side of Saint Andrews churchyard in Main Street, Thringstone. Mr Booth was a shipping line owner whose enquiries into the conditions of the London working class, and campaign for the introduction of old age pensions, helped lay the foundations of the modern welfare state.

He was born in Liverpool and married Mary Macaulay (cousin to Beatrice Potter) in 1871. They made Grace Dieu Manor their country residence in 1886 and hosted numerous gatherings there for family and friends until his death following a stroke in 1916. Mary remained at Grace Dieu until her death in 1939.

Cademan and Grace Dieu Wood are actively being expanded by their owners with the assistance of The National Forest Tender Scheme. The Sustrans Trail (52) through Grace Dieu Wood was developed as a cycle and all-abilities trail during 2000 as part of a national cycling network. Cademan Wood borders on Grace Dieu Wood and the circular Ivanhoe trail passes through part of the wood. The short section from Swannymote

Road to Thringstone of this trail is a pleasant woodland walk, linking up with Grace Dieu Trail 52. It passes close by the 'twenty steps' built during the days of Grace Dieu priory to the top of Temple Hill as part of the route of devotion.

WHITWICK

Whitwick and Thringstone lie on the Thringstone Fault, the dividing line between the Charnwood Forest rocky outcrops and the clay deposits of the coalfields.

Both these villages were mentioned in the Domesday Book (1086) but today a street sign in Loughborough Road is the only visible border between them. According to the entry in the Domesday Book the 'Manor of Witewic' belonged to Hugh de Grandmesnil and included Bardon, Markfield and other surrounding villages. There is evidence of a castle built between 1135 and 1154 and strengthened in the reign of King John (1199 – 1216), during which time the Manor of Whitwick most probably belonged to the king. Subsequent landlords did not make this castle their prime residence and today the name Castle Hill is the only reminder of its existence.

The Whitwick Colliery was only opened by William Stenson in 1826. It was the site of a major colliery fire in 1898 in which 35 miners lost their lives. The mine closed in 1986. A quarry outside Whitwick is still active, but hardly noticeable to traffic because of the trees planted around the site.

Twenty Steps to Temple Hill

In a bid to rejuvenate the village after closure of the local collieries, Whitwick developed the Hermitage Leisure Centre in Silver Street, offering a heated pool, gymnasium, indoor and outdoor sports facilities, including the Hermitage Lakeside municipal golf course and fishing.

Hermitage Leisure Centre, Whitwick

BARDON HILL AND BARDON

Bardon Hill is part of the Warren Hill range in Charnwood Forest. At 278 m (912 ft) it is the highest point in Leicestershire and for that matter, the highest point on a straight eastern line all the way to the Urals in Russia. It also offers great views to Sugar Loaf in South Wales, the Shropshire Hills, and summits in North Wales and Derbyshire. There is no open-access road leading up to the summit, but a footpath one mile long from the village of Copt Oak leads past Bardon Hall to the top.

The Bardon Hill quarry at the western side of the hill dates back to 1860 and is still an active hard rock quarry for road construction. Breedon Everard lived in Bardon Hall and had a summer house on top of the hill. He was responsible for Bardon and Billa Barra quarries and went on to become a well-known supplier of builders' material in Leicester.

Bardon has recently been developed into a major light industrial and warehousing centre. Its close proximity to the M1 made it the obvious choice for redevelopment and to offer alternative employment to the region after the closure of all the mines.

Views from the top of Bardon Hill:

Showing part of the quarry and the industrial developments in Bardon (top)

Towards the north (left)

BILLA BARRA

Just south of Bardon Hill off the B591 on the way to Stanton under Bardon, is Billa Barra. It is a disused quarry, obtained and developed in conjunction with the National Forest Company since 1996 into 18 ha (45 acres) of mixed grassland and newly planted woodland. Stones were mainly quarried for dry stone walls and the quarry has exposed rocky outcrops dating back to the Precambrian era, making it a Regionally Important Geological Site. The site offers parking and clearly marked walks to the top of the hill. From the top of the hill, other active and disused Cliffe Hill quarry sites are visible towards the south.

THORNTON RESERVOIR

Thornton Reservoir is a 30 ha (75 acre) reservoir, built in 1854, and was opened to visitors in 1997 by Severn Trent Water. It is set amongst rolling farmland and woodland with a well constructed all-abilities track around the water for walkers and cyclists. It also has large areas of shallow water where weed growth ensures good hatches

> The Thringstone Fault was created by prehistoric volcanic eruptions causing faulting in the underlying Paleozoic Rock. It runs from Ticknall to Bardon along the Warren Hill range and signifies the end of the coalfields

of insects, making it an ideal venue for birdwatching, batwatching and fishing (especially trout).

Fishing is allowed from February to November. An exhibition and fishing lodge, in the shape of a capsized boat, contains a tearoom and shop. Facilities for picnics and well positioned benches can be found around the lake. Also visit the garden centre, close to the resort for a good selection of local plants.

The Fishing Lodge at Thornton Reservoir (above)

Hiking around the Thornton Reservoir (left)

35

2 Coalfields

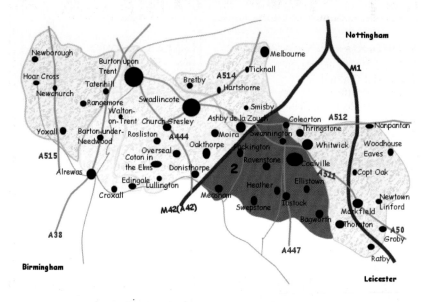

EXPLORE THE COALFIELDS IN TWO SECTIONS
- Medieval Coalfields (Swannington and Coleorton)
- Coalville and Mining Villages (Coalville to Packington)

Coal was known to exist to the west of the Thringstone Fault from before the 10th century. The coal in the seam around Coleorton and Swannington was near the surface and therefore mined from medieval times. This activity became so prolific that it became treacherous to walk outside at night unless you knew and stayed on the established footpaths, for fear of falling into a mine shaft. Today the area around Coleorton is still unique because of the warren of footpaths throughout the area.

Coalville and the southern coalfields, on the other hand, were developed during the 19th and 20th centuries. Coal deposits here were deep under the mudstone and it was only after the invention of the steam engine that it became feasible to mine this coal. All the mines closed by the middle of the 1980s and the area diversified into light industry and warehousing with an added emphasis on regeneration of the disused mining sites to nature reserves.

Information in Brief

Information Centres:

North West Leicestershire
District Council
Council Offices
Stenson Road, Coalville, LE67
3FJ
Tel: 01530 454545
e-mail:
regeneration@nwleicestershire.gov.uk
Website: www.nwleics.gov.uk

Coalville Tourist Information
Centre
Snibston Discovery Park,
Ashby Road, Coalville LE67 3LN
Tel: 01530 813608
e-mail:
coalville.tic@nwleicestershire.gov.uk
Website: www.nwleics.gov.uk

Woodlands and Parks:

Bagworth: Bagworth Heath
Wood, Royal Tigers Wood,
Centenary Wood
Coleorton: Coleorton Wood
Ibstock: Sence Valley Forest
Park

Lakes and Reservoirs:
Bagworth Heath lake (fishing)
Sence Valley Forest Park lake
(fishing)
Whitwick Hermitage Centre dam
(fishing)

Places of Interest:

Coalville: Snibston Discovery
Park, Donington le Heath Manor
House
Swannington: Railway Incline,
Hough Mill

Relevant Websites:
www.go-fish.co.uk
www.birdinguk.co.uk
www.swannington-heritage.co.uk
www.nationalforest.org

Newly developed Sence Valley Forest Park on the site of the disused mine

Medieval Coalfields

Situated in the heart of the Midlands Coal Seam, coal has been mined in this area since the 12th century. The resulting pattern of small irregular fields and a dense network of footpaths, is unique in Leicestershire. The first commercial railway to transport coal was built here by Robert Stephenson, son of George Stephenson of Stephenson's *"Rocket'* fame. The area was popular with painters and writers such as Wordsworth, the Beaumonts and Sir Walter Scott.

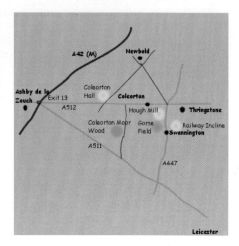

Directions

- Exit the M1 at Junction 23 and travel west toward Ashby de la Zouch on the A512, to the roundabout crossing with the A447
- Turn left on to the A447 for **Swannington** and the **Swannington Incline, the Hough Mill** and **Gorse Field**
- At the next roundabout of the A447 with the A511, turn right on to the A511 towards Ashby de la Zouch
- Turn right after Sinope towards **Coleorton** Moor for **Coleorton Wood**
- At the T junction with the A512, turn right back towards the A447 for a view over Coleorton from the car park of the George Inn to the left
- At the A447 roundabout turn first left towards Newbold for a drive through Coleorton
- At the T junction turn left into Rempstone Road. **Coleorton Hall** is on the right just before the junction with the A512
- Return to the M1 on the A512, or continue right, on the A512 to the A42 at junction 13.

SWANNINGTON AND HOUGH MILL

Swannington was first mentioned in 1205 when it was described in a charter of King John as the place 'where cole is gotten'. Since then the history of the village was closely linked to coal. It is a long winding village stretching along the A447 and is today predominantly a commuter residential village for surrounding towns.

Coal mining occurred at Swannington, first from the surface and outcrops, then from bell-pits, followed by shaft mining whose depths could only increase by the use of steam driven pumping and winding engines. Initially coal was transported to Leicester by pack mule up to the mid 18th century. With the construction of the Hinckley/ Melbourne Turnpike road (1760) the dominant mode of transport switched to carts.

In 1829, Robert Stephenson, the son of George Stephenson (of the 'Rocket' fame) was drafted in to design a railway system to transport coal from Swannington to Leicester. The railway was first opened in 1833 and was not only the first commercial railway in the UK, but also featured two inclines (at Bagworth and Swannington) where steam driven winding engines were used to lift full wagons and lower empty wagons along the steep inclines.

The winding engine used along the Swannington incline survived the closing of the Califat mine in 1873. A joint Pumping Company installed a huge twin steam engine in the former Swannington No 1 (Calcutta) mine to pump out water from the surrounding pits and the incline was used to transport fuel to this steam engine. Today this incline winding engine is housed in the National Railway Museum in York. The incline has been re-developed as part of the Village Trail by the Swannington Heritage Trust; their booklet is available at the local Post Office and shops.

> The first commercial railway line in the UK was built between Leicester and Swannington by Robert Stephenson in the 1830s.

View down the Swannington Incline

Site of the winding engine at the top of the Swannington incline

Swannington was also a centre for the milling industry of the region until the end of the 18th century. The Hough Mill is a recently restored brick tower (no sails or fantail) open to visitors on Sundays from April to September. The Mill was built by Mr Griffen in the late 18th century on the site of an older post mill, and is made up of four levels containing two pairs of millstones, stone floor machinery, mill related artefacts, exhibits and interpretation panels.

Next to the mill is the Gorse Field woodland nature reserve containing the remains of the Califat colliery, a 19th-century mine. It is the only remaining local area that has never been intensively farmed and therefore typical of the 12th century mining terrain.

Hough Mill seen from the Gorse Fields

COLEORTON AND MEDIEVAL COAL MINING

The landscape around Coleorton, Newbold and Griffydam was sculptured by medieval surface coal mining, dating back to the 13th century. It displays the mixed pattern of linear settlements, interspersed with the uneven remainder of bell pits and spoil heaps that can be associated with small scale mining. At the peak of the mining era during the late 18th century, up to 15 mines were active in this area and the footpaths were the only safe way to travel after dark, for fear of falling into a pit. The dense network of public footpaths is a stark reminder of this period. The landscape pattern is unique in Leicestershire and gives the area a character of intimacy as can be viewed from the car park of the George Inn on the A512. It is worth while taking a tour through some of the smaller hamlets such as Church Farm and Farm Town with their very narrow and winding lanes.

Coleorton Wood on Pit Lane in Coleorton Moor is the 6 ha (15 acre) reclaimed site of the 'Bug and Wink' colliery, opened in 1875 as the last mine in Coleorton. Rumour has it that miners used to stay away from work on hearing the sound of the Seven Whistlers or Golden Plowers bird, signifying potential disaster in the mine! After closure in the early 1930s, the site has been planted with mixed woodland and is open during daylight hours with paths and a car park.

Through the centuries Coleorton had strong links with literature and the arts. Coleorton Hall, on the A512, was the seat of the Leicestershire Beaumonts for more than 500 years. The Hall was regularly visited by celebrities like Wordsworth and Sir Walter Scott who apparently planned and wrote parts of his book, *Ivanhoe*, on a stone seat in the winter garden of Coleorton Hall. During the Civil War in the 17th century, the regional head-quarters of the Cromwellian forces was on the site of the hall. This allowed them to launch cannon balls towards the Royalist stronghold at Ashby Castle, two miles away. The current hall was completed by Sir Howland Beaumont in 1807. After his death in 1827 he was buried in the churchyard of St Mary's in Coleorton.

More recently, until the mid 1980s the regional Coal Board had its offices in the Hall. The Hall is currently being converted into private apartments. A Dame Margaret is said to haunt the grounds of Coleorton Hall and is supposed to rattle chains first in the house and then in the grounds every year on the 12th of March.

View of Coleorton from the George Inn (above)

Coleorton Hall overlooking the sprawling village of Coleorton (right)

Mining Techniques through the Centuries
Part 1 Surface Mining

OUTCROPPING

Outcropping is the earliest form of coal mining. Coal is picked up or dug out of shallow pits. The earliest local record of this type of mining is 1204 when the freemen of Swannington Common were given the right to mine for coal. It is believed that coal was mined earlier than this date in the Swannington and Coleorton areas. There is no evidence that adit mining (digging of coal out of hill site seams) was a common practice in The National Forest.

BELL PITS

As the digging for coal went deeper, bell pits became common from the 13th century onwards. In this method coal is dug out of the edges of deeper pits in a bell shape around the pit. These pits were usually dug close together so that the spoils from the latest pit can be used to fill up the older exhausted pit. Coal would have been carried out by ladders or hauled out by hand, restricting the depth of the pit.

USE OF WINDLASSES

The use of windlasses on bell pits during the 14th and 15th centuries allowed for deeper pits to be sunk as the coal, spoils and miners could be hauled out, rather than being restricted by the length of ladders. Evidence of this type of bell-pit mining can be found in small circular mounds of spoils and inverted bell-shaped depressions where the shafts collapsed.

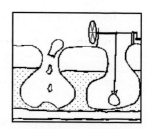

Coalville and Mining Villages

Coal was discovered under the clay along Long Lane (the current Ashby Road in Coalville) during the 18th century. This was a better quality coal, also referred to as the 'Leicester Bright' because of its shiny nature. It heralded the start of deep pit mining, the creation of new villages like Coalville, and the expansion of Whitwick, Ibstock and Ellistown as typical mining villages. Without mines the heathland of Measham and Packington to the west of Coalville, retained their rural character.

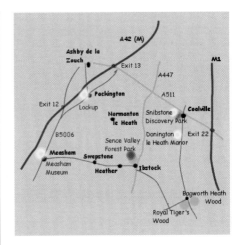

Directions

- Exit the M1 at junction 22 and turn west towards Coalville on the A511 to the A447 roundabout
- Take the turnoff towards **Coalville**. **Snibston Discovery Park** is on the right
- From the park, turn towards Coalville town centre and turn right into Belvoir Road for **Donington le Heath Manor House**
- Follow the signs to Ellistown and **Bagworth** for **Bagworth Heath Wood**, the **Royal Tigers Wood** and **Centenary Wood**
- Follow the signs to Ibstock on the A447 and the **Sence Valley Forest Park** outside Ibstock
- Turn west through Heather to **Measham**
- From Measham travel north on the B5006. Turn off before crossing the M42 motorway towards **Packington** and a possible detour to **Normanton le Heath**
- Exit on to the M42 from Packington.

COALVILLE AND SURROUNDING MINING VILLAGES

Coalville evolved as a village out of the necessity to house miners. In 1824 William Stenson bought land in Whitwick and opened Long Lane Colliery to mine the deep coal seam referred to as the Leicester Bright. His intention was to mine coal and use the clay from the diggings for a brickwork industry of firebricks and earthenware. His main problem was how to transport the coal and he persuaded Robert Stephenson, the son of George Stephenson (of the 'Rocket' fame), to construct Leicestershire's first railway (and the first commercial railway line in the UK). The railway line opened in 1833 between Leicester and Swannington via Coalville, and it became feasible to sink other mines such as Snibston 1 & 2. Houses were built to accommodate miners flocking to the area for work and by 1848 Coalville was the accepted name of the new settlement.

Passengers on the new railway line had to disembark at the foot of the Bagworth incline, walk to the top and embark again at the top. It is therefore understandable that the trains, even then, were not very punctual. By the end of the 19th century a Samuel Fisher narrated an incident where the journey from Leicester to Coalville was delayed for 45 minutes in Bardon to allow two passengers to complete a fist fight on the station platform, which had started during the journey!

Although Coalville thrived as a village during the second half of the 19th century, it remained split over four different parishes, each with different plans and priorities. By 1892 the civil parish of Whitwick was eventually dissolved and Coalville received recognition as a separate parish. Coalville went on to become the Urban District for the area and eventually the administrative centre for the District of North West Leicestershire in 1974. The Council Buildings of North West Leicestershire District Council are in the centre of Coalville.

This period of growth came to an end with the closure of the coalmines during the 20th century - Snibston 1 at the turn of the century, Snibston 2 in 1983 and Whitwick Colliery in 1986. Coalville had to change again to adapt. Its close proximity to the M1 and strategic location in the centre of England, made it attractive to warehousing and light industry. The Industrial/Business Parks in Bardon and along the A511 outside Coalville again brought prosperity to Coalville during the final decades of the 20th century.

Coalville town centre and two pubs

Snibston Discovery Park and Tourist Information Centre (above left). Sculptures at Snibston Discovery Park (above right)

The centre of Coalville around the Clock Tower is an excellent example of the old and the new in partnership. The Pick n' Shovel, the Red House and the Snibstone New Inn pubs are symbols of the strong mining heritage of the village, while the Council Building, library and the Belvoir Shopping Centre are proof of its readiness to embrace the future. The town Market Hall in the Belvoir Shopping Centre opens on Tuesdays, Fridays and Saturdays. One of Coalville's main attractions is the Snibston Discovery Park.

SNIBSTON DISCOVERY PARK

Snibston Discovery Park is a 40 ha (100 acre) all weather, science and industrial heritage park and museum built on the site of the former Snibston Number 2 Colliery. This award winning tourist attraction explores amongst other things the transport, mining, engineering and textile industries of Leicestershire. Hands-on activities, colliery tours by ex-miners, a play area and the nature reserve make it a popular destination for the whole family. There is a shop, café and toilet facilities and ample parking. Snibston Discovery Park also houses the main Tourist Information Centre for Coalville area.

Other facilities offered around Snibston include a golf course, fishing lake and walks to other historic mining sites in surrounding villages such as Swannington.

MINING VILLAGES

By 1880 Coalville boasted three coal mines and Whitwick had two. In addition, coal mines and quarries were operational in most of the surrounding villages, such as Ellistown, Heather, Ibstock, Bagworth and Ravenstone. The villages thrived and expanded to house the local and migrating miners and workers in secondary industries such as brickmaking. Robert Stephenson made his home in Ravenstone from 1833 to 1838 after the opening of the Leicester/Swannington railway.

As the mines started closing during the 20th century, redevelopment was spurred on by the light industry and service/business centres around Coalville, and the regeneration of the environment by the Councils, the National Forest Company projects and other trusts.

DONINGTON LE HEATH MANOR HOUSE

The Donington le Heath Manor House south of Coalville, was built around 1280 and renovated during the early 17th century. It has been restored as a 17th century period house and provides an excellent example of a medieval first-floor house. The garden contains period herb gardens and a miniature maze. The house is open all year round and monthly events are held to recreate Leicestershire history. The barn houses a tearoom and restaurant with a shop in the Manor House

Donington le Heath Manor House
Picnic and parking facilities at

BAGWORTH AND BAGWORTH HEATH WOODS

Bagworth's history, like Coalville and Swannington is linked to coal and the railway line developed by Robert Stephenson in the early 1830s. One of the two inclines where steam engines were used to lift full trucks and lower empty trucks of coal along the line, is situated near Bagworth (the second one is at Swannington). But more memorable is the fact that the steam engine whistle was a direct result from an accident near Bagworth. A newspaper cutting from a local newspaper stated:

> It was on Saturday, May 4th 1833, that there occurred an accident which gave us the engine whistle. It was on the level crossing between Bagworth and Thornton that driver Weatherburn drove the engine Samson into a market cart containing 50lbs of butter and 80 dozen eggs. So serious an affair was reserved for Stephenson's consideration. A meeting of directors was called, and the manager's suggestion of a whistle which steam can blow was adopted. He went at once to a musical instrument maker in Leicester, who constructed a 'Steam Trumpet' which ten days later was tried in the presence of the Board of Directors. In appearance it was alike a huntsman's horn, 18 inches long and 6 inches across at the top.

An incident near Bagworth led to the invention and manufacture of the first railway steam whistle

Bagworth Heath Wood

Bagworth Heath Wood between Bagworth and Thornton is the 75 ha (225 acre) reclaimed Desford colliery site, newly redeveloped into a woodland park and lake, for fishing and with walking trails.

Two young Woodland Trust developments border on Bagworth Heath Wood and offer good walks within the woods and to Thornton and Bagworth. The Royal Tigers Wood is a 6 ha (14 acre) native species woodland with small arboretum. Trees from all 17 countries where the Royal Leicestershire Regiment served, are represented in the

arboretum. Centenary Wood is a 11 ha (27 acre) broadleaf and shrubs park.

SENCE VALLEY FOREST PARK

The Sence Valley Forest Park between Heather and Ibstock, is another good example of the regeneration of a disused opencast mine. The 60 ha (150 acre) site includes new broadleaved and conifer woodland, lakes and grassland. It has a reputation as an excellent bird watching site especially during the winter months, with a hide overlooking grass and the lakes.

There are trails for walkers, cyclists, horse-riders and disabled visitors. Fishing is allowed at one of the lakes in the nature reserve. A car park with information boards and toilet facilities is available next to the A447.

New trees in Royal Tigers Wood (above) Walk in Sence Valley Forest Park (below)

HEATHER AND NORMANTON LE HEATH

The 'heath' in the names of Normanton le Heath, Heather and Donington le Heath implies an area of heathland around the River Sence. Historically this would have made it a preferred settlement area and relics from an iron age settlement were found near Normanton le Heath on its boundaries with Heather and Ravenstone. There is also some indication that a Roman road from Leicester to Chester could have passed through Normanton le Heath (then Moira and Willesley), as well as an earlier Salt Way from Measham.

MEASHAM

Named after the River Mease, Measham had many different spellings throughout the ages, such as Messeham in the Domesday Book. It was initially closely linked to the royal family of Mercia, based at Repton, but was laid waste by the armies of William the Conqueror. During the 12th and 13th century Measham thrived as a trading centre on the Salt Way, strategically positioned between the major centres of Birmingham, Leicester, Nottingham and Derby. Joseph Wilkes bought the manor house in 1780 and further developed these trade links during the industrial revolution. He also manufactured 'jumbricks' or 'gob bricks' – i.e. housebricks twice the size of normal bricks. As houses were taxed on the number of bricks, this meant lower taxes. Jumbricks are still visible in some of the older houses along High Street.

The museum in the High Street is open on Tuesdays and Saturday mornings from February to November. It contains Measham pottery and terracotta, known as Rockingham ware, distinctive brown glazed pottery covered with sprigs of leaves and birds.

Measham Museum (above)

Comparing jumbricks to standard bricks in the walls (left)

Measham was selected as the first model village for redevelopment in The National Forest, resulting in various projects, such as the new leisure centre for the village and the rewatering of the Ashby canal from Snarestone to Moira, via Measham.

Measham has its own ghost story about a cyclist wearing a flat cap, with a miner's bag on the handlebars, that disappears mysteriously at a crossroad. One theory is that it could have been a miner who was killed in Measham in 1940 during a blackout.

Roundhouses or lockups were introduced during the end of the 18th century as a response by villages to the problem of occasional troublemakers and transit prisoners. The small round building had no window and a sturdy oak door. Today only 200 remain in the country.

PACKINGTON

Packington is on the Gilwhiskaw Brook, a tributary of the Mease. The area was gifted to new Abbey of St Mary, Coventry in 1043 by Leofric. Though bordering on the coal fields, Packington never really had a high yield and the mines closed in the 1940s.

Holy Rood, the village church, dates back to the 13th century, but it was the resident vicar, Thomas Pestell, who caused the village to be caught in the middle between the Cromwellian garrison at Coleorton Hall and the Royalist regiment in Ashby Castle during the Civil War (17th century). Thomas Pestell, was a Royalist sympathiser and was often intimidated by the soldiers from the garrison.

Packington, together with Smisby and Ticknall, boast three of the 200 village lockups or roundhouses still remaining in the UK, used to retain prisoners in transit or local vagrants. The Packington lockup was gifted to the village of Packington by the Countess of Loundoun in 1997.

Village lockup in Packington

Mining Techniques through the Centuries— Part 2 Deep Mining

TIMBER LINED SHAFTS

The danger of bell pit mining is that the coal seam could only be worked for a short distance around the shaft because of the danger of a collapsing roof. In the Lounge open cast site in Coleorton it was however found that oak props were used as early as 1450 to strengthen the shaft and the digging chambers and to hold up the tunnel roofs. This is the oldest dated timber lined mine in Britain and allowed shafts as deep as 30 m (100) feet. A reconstruction of a medieval deep shaft mine can be seen at the Snibston Discovery Park.

REVOLVING WINCHES, HORSE GINS

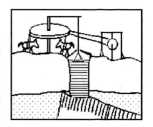

The 17th century saw improvements in the methods used to haul coal out to the surface. Large revolving winches were developed to replace the windlasses on the bell pits. These winches were initially powered by men, but by the 17th century horses were strapped to the wheels to provide the power, known as horse gins. Horse gins were commonly used in Coleorton and Swannington and the teams of horses and their minders rented by the day. The paths walked out by the horses however, often resulted in collapsed mineshafts.

INDUSTRIAL STEAM ENGINES

Water in the mines caused major problems in the late 17th century. Earlier solutions of dividing shafts and lighting a fire in one to cause a draft or removing water by using chain pumps became ineffective. Thomas Savery's 'Fire Engine' and especially the atmospheric steam engine developed by Newcomen in 1705 revolutionised the industry and the Newcomen engine was widely used in Coleorton and Swannington during the 18th century, replacing Horse Gins.

3 Coal and Clay

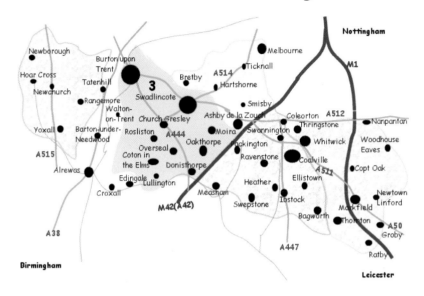

EXPLORE THIS AREA IN TWO SECTIONS:

- Around the Ashby Woulds (The heart of The National Forest)
- Further Afield (Linton to Netherseal)

Coal was always the primary natural resource in the Midlands, with clay from the pits used as secondary by-products. The Ashby Woulds and Lowlands surrounding the Woulds, however had the additional luxury of yielding not only coal, but also iron ore and a special high quality clay, all valuable commodities.

The inventions of the Industrial Revolution allowed these resources to be extracted economically and the region thrived. Furnaces, iron foundries, kilns and potteries opened in abundance, at the same time clearing the surrounding forests for more mines and wood to fuel the furnaces. Roads, canals and railway lines were built to transport the resources to other parts of the country and villages expanded to house the mine and industry workers. The loser during this period of wealth, was Nature.

During the second half of the 20th century most of the mines and earthworks started closing down. Either the natural resources ran out or became uneconomical to obtain. The destruction of the environment during the boom period, became one of the main motivational factors in the selection of a suitable location for the planned National Forest during the early 1990s. Moira, in the Ashby Woulds was selected as the home of the newly formed National Forest Company and their focus on regeneration.

The success of this regeneration is dramatic and clearly visible in the Coal and Clay area.

Information in Brief

Information Centres:

National Forest Company
Bath Lane,
Moira, Derbyshire DE12 6BD
Tel: 01283 551211
email: discover@nationalforest.org
Website: www.nationalforest.org

Ashby Tourist Information Centre
North Street, Ashby de la Zouch,
Leicestershire LE65 1HU
Tel: 01530 411767
email:
ashby.tic@nwleicestershire.gov.uk
Website: www.nwleics.gov.uk

South Derbyshire District Council
Civic Offices
Civic Way, Swadlincote,
Derbyshire DE11 0AH
Tel: 01283 595754
email: tourism@south-derbys.gov.uk
Website: www.south-derbys.gov.uk

Woodlands and Parks:

Coton in the Elms: Coton Wood
Church Gresley: Swainswood Park
Donisthorpe: Donisthorpe Woodland Park, Donisthorpe New Wood, Saltersford Valley Picnic area
Linton: Foxley Wood, Long Close and Top Wood
Moira: Conkers, Sarah's Wood
Netherseal: Grangewood
Oakthorpe: Oakthorpe Wood
Rosliston: Rosliston Forestry Centre, Beehive Farm
Swadlincote: Swadlincote Woodland Park,
Willesley: Willesley Wood

Canals, Lakes and Reservoirs:

Ashby Canal, Moira (boating)
Willesley lake (fishing)

Places of Interest:

Grangewood Zoo
Moira: Conkers Adventure Centre, Moira Furnace
Swadlincote: Dry Ski Slope, Green Bank Leisure Centre, Shopping Precinct

Relevant Websites

www.go-fish.co.uk
www.birdinguk.co.uk
www.forestry.gov.uk
www.visitconkers.com
www.skihoo.co.uk

Around the Ashby Woulds

It is the smallest but was once the most highly industrialised area in Leicestershire which resulted in serious scarring of the environment. Today it forms the heart of The National Forest, being actively transformed into pleasant woodlands for all to enjoy.

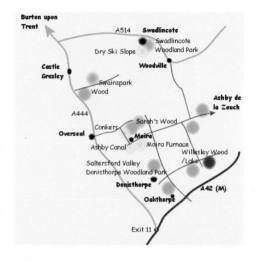

Directions

- Exit the M42 at junction 11 and take the A444 towards Burton upon Trent
- At Overseal turn right and follow the signs to The National Forest **Visitor Centre** in Moira for **Conkers** and **Sarah's Wood**
- Drive into **Moira** for the **Moira Furnace** and the **Ashby Canal**
- Turn right towards **Oakthorpe. Donisthorpe Wood** and **Saltersford Valley Park** are to the right. Return to Donisthorpe
- At the crossing in Donisthorpe turn right into Ashby Road to **Oakthorpe Wood** and picnic area, **Willesley Wood** and **Willesley Lake**
- Turn left towards Norris Hill passing developing woodland on the right and earthworks to the left, and join the Moira/Ashby road for a short distance
- Turn left via Blackfordby and Woodville to **Swadlincote** for the **Dry Ski Slope, Swadlincote Woodland Park** and the **Potteries**
- From Swadlincote take the A514 to the A444 and left to the M42 past Castle Gresley. Detour to **Swainspark**
- Return to the M42 on the A444 at junction 11.

ASHBY WOULDS

Ashby Woulds include the district of Moira, Albert Village, Spring Cottage and nearly 60 ha (143 acre) of Bootthorpe. It was once the most highly industrialised area in Leicestershire. The Rawdon, Moira, Marquis and Hastings coal mines were sunk by Frances Rawdon-Hastings, the 2nd Earl of Moira, in the early 19th century. Of these the Rawdon pit reached a depth of 305m (1000 ft) by 1868. At the same time the clay in Ashby Woulds was the best of its kind in the UK and when prepared, was one of the toughest, most resistant and non-corrosive materials used in the clay industry. Moira Pottery, established in 1922, produced jam jars, containers and clay used by educational and art schools all over Britain. The pottery closed in 1980 and the site was transformed into a 16 ha (40 acre) woodland of 40,000 newly planted trees.

Today the emphasis in the Ashby Woulds is on the transformation of these former open cast mines, quarries and industrial sites into new and/or renovated woodlands with well laid out trails for hiking, cycling, riding and other visitor attractions.

CONKERS

Moira is the home of the National Forest Company. It has its offices on the outskirts of the village and next to Conkers, its information and adventure centre. Conkers in Rawdon Road, offers a memorable day out for the whole family as it features outdoor activities such as an assault course, sculpture trails, train rides and canopy walks in its 45 ha (120 acres) of woodland. Indoor activities include feeling how a leaf breathes or seeing the world through the eyes of a bat. The lakeside restaurant is very popular.

Conkers outdoor activity park and train

Other developments around Moira include Sarah's Wood and the Ashby Canal. Sarah's Wood is a 10 ha (25 acre) site transformed into a woodland as a haven for wildlife. The play area is specifically designed for children with special needs and the park includes a 1 km (100 yd) tarmac all-abilities footpath around the site.

Conkers Visitor Centre (left)

MOIRA

Historically Moira Baths was well known for its beneficial cure against rheumatism during the 19th century. Thomas Cook took advantage of this and arranged tours to the Ivanhoe Baths and Royal Hotel in Ashby de la Zouch with water from Moira. The coal and clay mines around Moira and the furnace to process iron ore from the mines, were the main industries during the late 19th and early 20th centuries.

MOIRA FURNACE

Today the Moira Furnace is a direct reminder of the area's heritage. It is an iron blast furnace on the banks of the Ashby Canal built by Francis Rawdon-Hastings, the 2nd Earl of Moira in 1804, and was a forerunner to later more advanced furnaces. The iron ore was however of poor quality and the furnace closed in 1812. Now set up as a museum, it offers hands-on activities and information on the workings of the furnace and the history of the area. The museum includes an engine house, lime kilns, a children's play area, tearoom and craft workshops.

Moira Furnace on the Ashby Canal (left)

"Little Smelters" playground at Moira Furnace (below)

ASHBY CANAL

The Ashby Canal opened in 1804 to transport coal and clay by horse drawn boat for 40 km (30 miles) from Spring Cottage on the Ashby Woulds to Marston on the Coventry Canal. Subsidence resulted in progressive breaches and partial closure of the canal in 1944, 1957, and eventually all the way north of Snareston in 1966.

One of the projects of the National Forest Company is to restore and re-water the full length of the canal. The 2.4 km (1.5 miles) of canal between Conkers and Moira Furnace has already been completed. In 1999 Moira Furnace Museum Trust purchased a canal barge constructed in 1908 and used on the Birmingham Canal Navigations. Initially a 32m (70 ft) Day Boat (horse drawn and able to return without turning), it was shortened into a 18m (39 ft) pleasure boat in 1976, repaired to the original riveted iron hull and rebuilt as a Stewart and Lloyds tug from the 1950s. Pleasure trips are arranged during the summer and there is a popular walk along the towpath of the canal from the Furnace to Conkers.

Lake in Saltersford Valley Park (right)

Barge on the Ashby Canal (below)

DONISTHORPE AND OAKTHORPE

Donisthorpe, as a parish, was only formed in 1838 from the civil parishes of Church Gresley, Measham, Stretton-en-le-Field, Ashby and Seal. Signs of settlements during the Neolithic age were found near Donisthorpe, and during Roman times major trading routes passed near the town from Leicester to Chester. In the Domesday Book the area was stated as belonging to William de Ferrers while Oakthorpe was referred to as a waste land.

The main industries of the towns were collieries and lime-works on the Ashby Woulds and farming wheat, barley and oats. Disused mines were re-developed during the latter part of the 20th century into woodland areas, all offering excellent walks.

Donisthorpe Woodland Park is 20 ha (50 acre) of new woodland on the former colliery site. The park offers 3 km (1.9 miles) of multi-purpose surfaced paths and links to other trails through the Ashby Woulds.

Oakthorpe Wood and picnic area was developed on the site of the disused Oakthorpe colliery and offers all-abilities walks and picnic facilities

Saltersford Valley between Donisthorpe and Oakthorpe is a 6 ha (15 acre) woodland planted around two mining subsidence sites and recommended for birdwatching and dragonflies near the water. In 1994/5 it won the Forestry Authority Centre of Excellence award. The wood features sculptures, meadowland, a lake, picnic area and all-weather trails. Walks link Saltersford Valley to Willesley Wood.

WILLESLEY

Willesley is situated in the floor of the Shell Brook. There are signs of a Roman road from Leicester which separates Willesley from Measham and Oakthorpe. Furthermore it was described in the Domesday Book as a wasteland, possibly because of the destruction of the village by the armies of William the Conqueror on his way along the Trent Valley.

Willesley Wood is a 40 ha (100 acre) Woodland Trust development, planted in 1991 on reclaimed land, including woodland, lake and meadows, making it one of the first sites to be developed as part of The National Forest. The surfaced path from the Oakthorpe picnic area and car park is suitable for disabled visitors. To the east of the wood is a man-made lake formed by mining subsidence and popular for carp fishing. The lake depth varies from inches to around 4 meters (12 feet) and tickets for fishing can be bought on the banks. A large part of the Willesley estate which used to be home to the powerful Hastings family of mining fame, is now a private golf course next to the lake.

WOODVILLE

The village of Woodville next to Swadlincote, grew around a wooden toll booth on the route from Liverpool to London, initially referred to as the Wooden Box. The village was officially renamed Woodville in 1847. It was known for the white clay dug out nearby and had several potteries and manufacturers of heavy clay goods, some of which are still around today. It was also the home of a major brewery (Brunt, Bucknall & Co), the building of which is still used for other purposes.

Fishing at Willesley Lake

SWADLINCOTE

Swadlincote is the largest town in the south west corner of Derbyshire and borders on Leicestershire and Staffordshire. It grew out of the need to support the area's mining, pottery and brick industries during the 19th and early 20th centuries. Today most of these have been replaced by engineering and service industries.

Most of the old colliery spoil heaps and clay works have been redeveloped into woodland, park-lands and activity centres around the outskirts of the town. The Swadlincote Woodland Park opposite the Dry Ski Slope was developed next to a new residential area, offering parking, toilet facilities, a popular children's play area and all-abilities walk through the newly planted park

Swadlincote also offers a well equipped leisure centre and a superb dry ski slope for skiers and snow boarders. The Green Bank Leisure centre offers swimming, squash, gym and more, while the all weather Dry Ski Slope includes a nursery slope, 160m (175 yd) main run and 650m (710 yd) toboggan run. The ski centre arranges various events throughout the year on the run and in its Alpine restaurant.

Learn to ski on Derbyshire's dry ski slope in Swadlincote

Nursery Ski Slope at Swadlincote (left)

Entrance to Swadlincote Woodland Park (left)

Playground at Swadlincote Woodland Park (below)

Swadlincote has very good shopping facilities, including a pedestrianised area and two potteries. Sharpe's Pottery dates back to the early 19th century and is today a registered museum and visitor centre. The Pottery produced pipes and toilets for local and export markets (especially the United States). View their interesting range of local pottery, including fancy loos and the typical blue and white striped Cornish Ware, manufactured by TG Green potteries. The Jungle Madness is a popular indoor play area for children.

CHURCH GRESLEY, CASTLE GRESLEY

The names of Castle Gresley and Church Gresley together with Drakelow can be linked back to the Gresley family who in 974 were gifted this area for their role in the Norman victory at the battle of Hastings. Nigel de Toeni, as he was then known, held this territory with the assistance of Henry de Ferrers, who helped him quell uprisings from locals. By the 11th century the family added Gresley to their name and built a castle at Castle Gresley (on Castle Knob). Church Gresley got the name when the family founded an Augustinian priory dedicated to St George on the site of the current parish church of St George and St Mary. The family made Drakelow Hall near Castle Gresley their residence until it was auctioned in 1933 and since then demolished (now the site of Drakelow Power Station).

The main industries of the village used to be coal mining and potteries. The redeveloped Ivanhoe railway line (now renamed as The National Forest Rail Link) between Leicester and Burton upon Trent is used for commercial transport and possibly in the future again for passengers. Swainspark Wood at the edge of Swainspark Industrial Estate and south of Church Gresley has already been redeveloped in a woodland park on reclaimed land.

Further Afield

An extension of the regeneration of mining and earthwork sites, the villages on the outskirts of the Ashby Woulds offer more established and newly developed woodland parks and forests. Sites around Rosliston and Grangewood offer something for every member of the family.

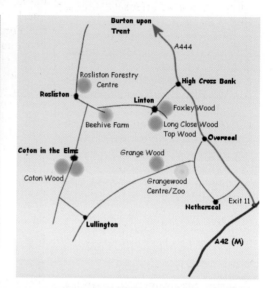

Directions

- Exit the M42 at junction 11 and take the A444 towards Burton upon Trent, past Overseal to the roundabout at High Cross Bank
- Turn left to **Linton** for **Foxley Wood**, **Long Close** and **Top Woods**
- In Linton take the road to **Rosliston** for the **Rosliston Forestry Centre** and **Beehive Farm Centre**
- From Rosliston drive to **Coton in the Elms** for **Coton Wood** and then on to **Lullington**
- Take the road towards Overseal from Lullington to **Grangewood**
- Turn off to **Netherseal** and rejoin the A444 again at Acresford
- Rejoin the M42 at junction 11.

LINTON

Although not as intensely mined, this area had its fair share of earthworks and therefore benefited from the re-forestation programmes of the Woodland Trust and The National Forest. Linton is home to two Woodland Trust developments.

Foxley Wood near Linton is a 28 ha (70 acre) Woodland Trust park mainly broadleaved woodland, offering good views with parking and an information board on site.

Long Close and Top Wood, is a further 80 ha (200 acres) Woodland Trust development of newly planted woodland, ponds, open grassland with footpaths and bridleways.

ROSLISTON

Rosliston has always been a farming community, mentioned in the Domesday Book as Redlauseton, probably meaning the farm of Hrolf (a Norseman). Today the village has become part of the commuter belt for Burton and Derby, but still manages to retain its agricultural character.

Rosliston Forestry Centre was developed as a collaboration between South Derbyshire District Council, the Forestry Commission and the National Forest Company into a 62 ha (154 acre) young woodland. Its trails are clearly marked, one of which is an all-abilities trail. The centre specialises in children's parties and family outings, offering an outside play area, including a popular sparrow-hawk climbing frame, and an inside soft play room. It is recognised as a good birding site, including a hide, and Birds of prey displays can be arranged for groups. Other facilities include crazy golf, bike hire and the new barn shop.

The Chapmans Nursery opposite the Centre stocks bedding plants, flowers and pot plants.

View from the bird-hide at Rosliston Forestry Centre (above)

Sparrowhawk climbing frame at Rosliston Forestry Centre (left)

Family outing at the Hen House, Beehive Farm Centre! (left)

Lullington Church (below)

Beehive Farm Centre features a 26 ha (65 acre) area of new woodland, lakes and meadows. It offers a 25 pitch caravan and camp site, trails for walkers and horseriders, fishing lakes, including facilities for disabled fishing, and an outdoor play area. Permits are required for fishing and horseriding. The farmhouse tea room, 'Hen House' and farm yard animals are popular, as are the pet and pony store, tack shop and collectables shops.

COTON IN THE ELMS

Coton was situated on a traditional trading route. In the Domesday Book it was mentioned as Cotune, held by Burton Abbey apparently on condition that the Abbey provided a hound on a leash to the king when he visited Derbyshire. The Elms part of the name refers to the Elm trees which used to frame all the roads into the village. Unfortunately these trees died of the Dutch Elm disease during the middle of the 20th century. The main industries were mining and agriculture.

The White House near Coton has the unusual name of 'Lad's Grave'. This could be a reference to Philip Greensmith, a soldier who was hanged for desertion in 1644 at Overfields Farm, Coton. The present church was built in 1846, but was preceded by a much older church originally built behind the current Shoulder of Mutton pub. It is believed that when this older church fell into disrepair, the bells went to the church in the neighbouring village, Lullington, so that the residents of Coton can still hear them on a Sunday morning if the wind is right.

Coton Wood, between the two villages, is a 33 ha (82 acre) Woodland Trust development of mainly broadleaved woodland and grassland with good views. It has an information board and car parking facilities on site and is worth a visit.

LULLINGTON

Lullington is an attractive village, mentioned as Lullitune in the Domesday Book. Farming and some mining were the main occupations for the villagers. One of the Salt Ways, possibly a minor Roman Road, is supposed to have passed through the village.

GRANGEWOOD

Grangewood Farm is a 40 ha (100 acre) broadleaf and conifer Woodland Trust park planted in 1997. The wood offers walks, fishing and horse-riding. The local livery centre welcomes holiday livery.

The Grangewood Garden Centre, situated in the Walled Garden of Grangewood Hall offers various garden products, craft rooms, pine furniture, acquatics and a tea room.

Grangewood Zoo is a 0.8 ha (2 acre) home for tropical birds, mammals, reptiles and insects. The zoo specialises in children's birthday Safari parties in their African Lodge and also gives regular talks on the natural habitat and way of life of the animals in the zoo.

OVERSEAL, NETHERSEAL

The name Seal suggests that the area was once heavily forested and in the Domesday Book these areas were described as a wooded area on the edge of the Ashby Woulds. Trading routes ran through the parish from Croxall to Acresford and its three manors were split amongst various owners, including the Gresley family. The Gresley family owned the land until the early 18th century, by which time William de Ferrers was the sole owner.

Although part of Overseal was closer to the Ashby Woulds' high yield coal fields, it was Netherseal that had a two shaft colliery sunk in 1867. The mine maintained its output in the late 19th century, by being the first mine in South Derbyshire to use an underground haulage system working on compressed air. Mining and related industries turned Netherseal into a thriving mining town during the 19th century. The centre of the village is now a conservation area with many listed buildings such as the Grade II listed Old Hall Hotel dating to around 1644. The cemetery is also the resting place of Sir Nigel Gresley, an engineer who designed the locomotive The Mallard, famous for setting the world speed record for a steam engine at 126 mph for a few seconds in 1938.

> The grave of Sir Nigel Gresley, the designer of the record-breaking Mallard steam engine is in Netherseal.

New forest planting on Grangewood Farm

4 Parklands and Reservoirs

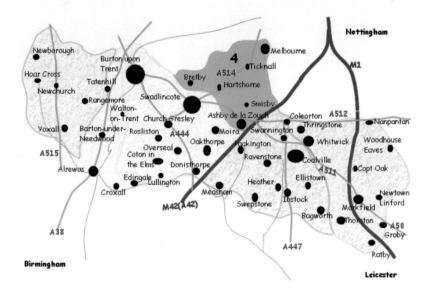

EXPLORE THE PARKLANDS IN THREE SECTIONS

- Ashby de la Zouch
- Country Parks and Manors (from Lount to Calke Abbey)
- Reservoirs (from Staunton Harold Reservoir to Bretby)

The arrival of the Saxons in the eighth century and the Norman invasion in the 11th century, heralded the distribution of land by the kings to trusted warrior nobles. Although the land was subdivided and changed hands over the centuries, this system of ownership had the advantage of enclosing large tracts of land as parkland, thereby preventing total deforestation in the areas with little natural resources.

The region from Melbourne to Ashby de la Zouch is an example of well preserved parklands in The National Forest. Large estates like Melbourne, Staunton Harold, and Calke Abbey retained their woodland characteristics and offer great days out.

In addition to the large estates, Staunton Harold and Foremark Reservoirs were built during the 19th and 20th century in the valleys. Very popular with local boating and fishing clubs, the reservoirs offer water activities, good children's play areas, bird watching opportunities and walks.

Information in Brief

Information Centres:

Ashby Tourist Information Centre
North Street, Ashby de la Zouch,
Leicestershire LE65 1HU
Tel: 01530 411767
email:
ashby.tic@nwleicestershire.gov.uk
Website: www.nwleics.gov.uk

South Derbyshire District Council
Civic Offices
Civic Way, Swadlincote,
Derbyshire DE11 0AH
Tel: 01283 595754
email: tourism@south-derbys.gov.uk
Website: www.south-derbys.gov.uk

Coalville Tourist Information Centre
Snibston Discovery Park, Ashby Road,
Coalville LE67 3LN
Tel: 01530 813608
email:
Coalville.toc@nwleicestershire.gov.uk
Website: www.nwleics.gov.uk

Woodlands and Parks:

Foremark: Carver's Rocks
Hartshorne: Nether Hall Wood
Lount: Lount Nature Reserve

Smisby: Woodcote, Bluebell Arboretum
Staunton Harold: Springwood, Dimminsdale

Canals, Lakes and Reservoirs:

Foremark Reservoir (boating, fishing)
Staunton Harold Reservoir (boating, fishing)

Places of Interest:

Ashby de la Zouch: Castle ruins, Museum, Mill Lane Mews
Calke Abbey
Melbourne and Melbourne Hall
Staunton Harold: Church, Ferrers Centre for Arts and Crafts

Relevant Websites:

www.nationaltrust.org.uk
www.nationalforest.org
www.theheritagetrail.co.uk
www.shsc.org.uk
(Staunton Harold Sailing Club)
www.birdinguk.co.uk
www.go-fish.co.uk

Red Deer in the grounds of Calke Abbey

Ashby de la Zouch

Situated at the edge of the coal fields, Ashby was a play-ground for Londoners who flocked in to visit its mineral baths during the Victorian era. Sir Walter Scott however put the town on the map by using its castle and surrounding area for the jousting scenes in his novel *Ivanhoe*.

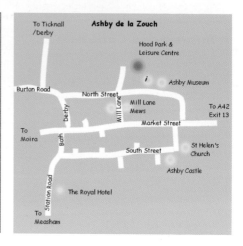

Directions

- Exit the A42 at junction 13 for **Ashby de la Zouch** and **Smisby**

Ruins of the Ashby de la Zouch Castle

ASHBY DE LA ZOUCH

The name of Ashby is derived from the Saxon 'aesc' meaning 'ash' and 'byr' meaning 'habitation'. In 1160 the de la Zouch was added to mark the transfer through marriage of the property to Alain Parrhoet la Zouch from Brittany. Although there is little evidence of a Roman Settlement near Ashby, Money Hill Farm between Ashby and Smisby received its name from two brass urns filled with Roman coins found there in 1818.

Shops in Mill Lane Mews

Ashby de la Zouch used to be famous as a spa town during the 19th century, with water containing medicinal qualities transported from Moira. In 1822 the Ivanhoe Baths were built and made popular with the nearby Hastings Hotel, through tours arranged by Thomas Cook from Melbourne. The hotel changed its name after a visit from the Dowager Queen Adelaide in 1839, to the Royal Hotel, as it is still known today. The baths closed in 1884 but Springs Health farm near Ashby is a reminder of this era and offers special holidays using its local springs and spa facilities.

Over the years Ashby retained its appearance of a market town. In the main street there are Elizabethan half-timbered houses alongside Georgian bow-fronted shops. Mill Lane Mews has been restored and contains a row of period shops, for which the designer received the coveted Europa Nostrom Award.

The museum in North Street has been a winner of the County Heritage Award in the past and is open from April to August. It contains interesting displays on the local history, including a model of the castle under siege, and information on Sir William Hastings, the Civil War, and French prisoners of war. It offers full access and facilities for disabled visitors, and books on the local history can be purchased it its shop.

Royal Hotel (above)

Ashby de la Zouch Museum (below)

Another interesting feature is the finger pillory in St Helen's Church which was in use until the early 1900s as a punishment for anyone interrupting the sermons.

Today Ashby de la Zouch is a prosperous commuter town for Birmingham, Derby, Nottingham and Leicester, with its own thriving light industry sector and an excellent range of shops. It however, still keeps its link with the past in the annual Ashby Statutes Fair, held in September, since receiving the charter from Henry III in 1219.

ASHBY CASTLE

It was however, mainly the castle in South Street that put Ashby de la Zouch on the map. The Castle was originally built as a hall in the 12th century with the large residential Warwick tower added during the 15th century. In 1474 Edward IV granted a fortification licence for the castle to Lord William Hastings, as a precaution against a siege. Lord Hastings added the Hastings Tower and a chapel and during the reign of Edward IV he rose to Lord Chamberlain as reward for his loyalty during the War of the Roses. However he refused to support Richard III after Edward's death in 1483, and was beheaded as a traitor, an event portrayed as a scene in Shakespeare's Richard III. The Countess of Huntingdon who led a religious revival in the 18th century was buried in this Hastings Chapel.

During the Civil War in the 17th century, Ashby de la Zouch Castle was the Royalist stronghold under Henry Hastings (later Lord Loughborough) against the Cromwellian forces who had their regional headquarters at Coleorton Hall, two miles away. The Royalists surrendered after a year long siege in 1646. There are rumours of battle cries and the clash of metal on metal being heard along Corkscrew Lane between Ashby and Coleorton, on the spot of a violent Civil War clash! The Castle is open daily from April to September and on Wednesdays, and Sundays from October to March.

After a period of decay, the castle was again brought to attention as the setting of a jousting tournament in Sir Walter Scott's novel *Ivanhoe* in 1820.

Ashby Castle played a significant role in the Civil War and was used as the setting for a jousting tournament in Sir Walter Scott's novel Ivanhoe.

Ruins of Ashby Castle

SMISBY

Smisby is an ancient farming settlement, the name probably derived from 'Smith's Farm'. It is linked to Ashby through Sir Walter Scott's novel *Ivanhoe*, referring to a field just outside Smisby as the jousting field for the knights:

> on the verge of a wood which approached within a mile of the town Ashby, was an extensive meadow, of the finest and most beautiful green turf … the ground … sloped gradually on all sides to a level bottom.

Smisby, together with Ticknall and Packington, has one of the remaining 200 round houses or lockups in which prisoners were held on their way to Derby. It is also the birthplace of Hannah Bailey, who with her husband Charles Baker went as missionaries to New Zealand in 1828 and helped to broker an agreement between the Maories and the settlers.

The Chapel of Ease in the church of St James dates back to 1068. It was constructed by monks from Repton and incorporated in the church by Ann Comyn (Lady of the Smisby Manor) during the 14th century. A memorial to Ann Comyn, monuments to the Kendalls, and oak panelling supposedly from Ashby Castle can still be seen in the church.

Woodcote is a 9.5 ha (23.5 acre) broad leaved Woodland Trust development with parking and information boards. It offers good views.

The Bluebell Arboretum and Nursery in Annwell Lane, Smisby offers a fine collection of rare trees, shrubs and plants on display and for sale.

Entrance to the Bluebell Arboretum (above)

Smisby Lockup and St James Church (left)

Country Parks and Manors

Many of the influential landowners made their homes in this pleasant parkland over the centuries. The area was originally used for hunting and therefore kept protected from industries and mining activities. Today the towns and villages offer business parks and are popular residential areas within the commuter belt of the nearby cities.

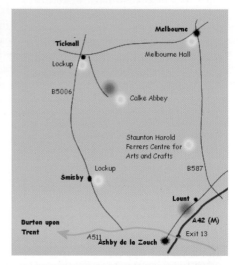

Directions

Exit the A42 at junction 13 towards Ashby de la Zouch
- At the roundabout turn right on to the B587 and pass the **Lount Nature Reserve** on the left
- Turn left towards Melbourne. **Staunton Harold** is on the left
- From **Melbourne** take the B587 to **Ticknall** and follow the signs to **Calke Abbey**
- Return to Ashby de la Zouch on the B5006 and rejoin the A42 at junction 11.

Summer display in the walled garden of Calke Abbey

LOUNT NATURE RESERVE

The New Lount colliery closed in 1968 and the colliery and tip site was acquired by Leicestershire County Council in 1997 to be managed by the Leicestershire and Rutland Wildlife Trust as a Local Nature Reserve. The 20 ha (50 acres) reserve now provides habitat in mature woodland, grassland and ponds to a wide variety of birds and animals.

STAUNTON HAROLD

Harold was a Saxon owner, but William the Conqueror gave the estate to Henry de Ferrers, a well known name in the history of The National Forest. The first hall at Staunton Harold was built by Sir William de Staunton in 1324. In 1423 Sir Ralph Shirley, the constable of Melbourne Castle, married into the family and made Staunton Hall the family home.

Sir Robert Shirley, the 1st Earl of Ferrers, rebuilt the house and added the church during the Common-wealth Period in 1653. The current Hall is a Georgian structure with a Palladian façade, designed and built in 1763 by the 5th Earl of Ferrers. It remained in the Ferrers family until its sale in 1954 to Group Captain Leonard Cheshire as a Sue Ryder Home for the Incurably Sick, and in 2002 to private owners, not open to the public. The Holy Trinity Church on the estate was obtained by the National Trust and is open to the public all year round. Its interior retained the original cushions, fine panelling and painted ceiling. The following interesting inscription can be found above the west door:

In the yeare 1653 when all things sacred were throughout ye nation either demolished or profaned, Sir Robert Shirley Barronnet, founded this church, whose singular praise it is to have done the best thinges in ye worst times and hoped them in the most callamitous. The righteous shall be had in ever-lasting remembrance.

Ferrers Centre for Arts and Craft (above)

Staunton Harold Hall and Church (left)

The Ferrers Centre for Arts and Crafts, in the Georgian courtyard next to the Hall, is home to a community of arts and crafts workshops, a tearoom and gift shop. The location is open all year round from Tuesdays to Sundays, and also features the prestigious Ferrers Gallery.

The Hall is surrounded by large parkland, woods and lakes, including nurseries and a large garden centre with unusual trees, shrubs and an aquatic centre. The Hall has recently been sold to private owners but the Church, Ferrers Centre and access to the grounds and pond next to the Church remain open to the public.

MELBOURNE

Melbourne is a fine example of a Georgian town centre in which much investment has been made in recent years to return it to its original appearance. It has thriving light industrial centres and offers a fine range of places to shop, eat, drink and stay. A booklet is available from local newsagents and the church as a walking guide through the town.

The name Melbourne is derived from the 'mill on the Brook' and was described in the Domesday Book as a royal manor. In 1311 Robert de Holand was given a licence to fortify Melbourne house into a castle, which was however never completed, and was demolished in the early 17th century. Some remains of the castle can still be seen on Castle farm by special arrangement with the owner of the farm. One of the most notorious prisoners in this castle was John,

Duke of Bourbon, the most important French prisoner taken at the battle of Agincourt in 1415, who was held in the castle for 19 years.

Melbourne Hall is a graceful and elegant mansion dating back to the early 17th century. It was once the home of the Victorian Prime Minister, William Lamb (1779 – 1848), who, as the 2nd Viscount of Melbourne, in 1837 gave permission for a 'tiny' settlement in Australia to be named after him! Lady Caroline Lamb, Byron's friend, used to be a resident of the Hall. The Lamb Inn keeps the memories of the Lamb family alive.

The Hall, now owned by the Marquis of Lothian, stands in formal gardens built in 1704 with the assistance of royal gardener, Henry Wise, in the manner of Le

The Lamb Inn, Melbourne (above)

The pool in front of Melbourne Hall (below)

Notre's gardens at Versailles. The garden also features a lake and fine examples of ironwork by the Derby ironsmith Robert Bakewell, such as the ornamental pergola known as the Birdcage. The pool was originally the mill pool for the hall's mill and is a favourite with families. The Hall is open to the public during August on Tuesdays to Saturdays, and the garden from April to September.

Another fine feature in the town is the parish church dedicated to St Michael with St Mary. It was built around 1120, is known as a cathedral in miniature and is a fine example of Norman architecture. During the middle ages it was the southern refuge for the Bishops of Carlisle, during which time they used the Hall as their rectory.

Thomas Cook who started popular travel in England, was born in Melbourne in 1808 and started his business there by arranging trips to the seaside. The Thomas Cook Memorial Cottages in Melbourne were built by him around 1890/91, consisting of 14 cottages, a bakehouse, laundry and a Mission hall. These are still used as accommodation for senior citizens.

TICKNALL

The village of Ticknall was recorded in the early 11ᵗʰ century as Ticenheale. It belonged to the estate of Calke Abbey until recent years. This strong link with the Harpur family of Calke Abbey is apparent in the seven almshouses which were built as monument to the family in 1772 after the death of Charles Harpur. Cast iron standpipes were also erected on

instructions of Sir Vauncey Harpur Crewe in 1914 to help villagers who previously had to fetch water from the springs.

Ticknall, like Smisby, features one of the 200 remaining roundhouses or lockups in England. It was built in 1809 as an overnight facility for prisoners in transit, with a secondary purpose to shelter drunks, paupers and vagrants. During World War II it was used as an arms storage.

The Church of St George, near the lockup, was built in 1831 on the site of the former church of Thomas a Beckett. Parts of the old church however proved to be resistant to the explosives used, and are still standing in the church yard. Much of the village today is a declared conservation area.

> Thomas Cook was born in Melbourne and started his package travel business from there.

Ticknall Lockup

Church of St George and ruin of the old church in Ticknall

CALKE ABBEY

The most interesting attraction is however Calke Abbey owned by the Harpur family from 1660 to 1985, and described as a 'time capsule where time stood still as during Queen Victoria's time'. It is one of the great houses of Derbyshire, second in size only to Chatsworth. The first baroque mansion house and park was built around 1701 – 1704 by Sir John Harpur in 240 ha (600 acres) of parkland and woodland. In 1808 Sir Henry Harpur added the Crewe to the name and started showing signs of eccentricity, as did his great grandson, Sir Vauncey Harpur Crewe during the 19/20th centuries. Both were reclusive, compulsive collectors and were fascinated by natural history as evidenced by the collection of stuffed animals and birds. The family threw nothing away, but stored their treasures in closed rooms. When Sir Vauncey's grandson sold the house to the National Trust in the 1980s it was virtually unchanged from when Sir Vauncey inherited it in 1886.

The exhibits in the house portray a Victorian country house in decline interspersed with real treasures such as the Chinese silk State Bed, probably made for George I in 1715 and which was still packed in its original box in 1985.

The Calke Abbey gardens feature a family chapel, restored orangery, formal and physic gardens. The estate also has a licensed restaurant and counter service for coffees and teas. The house is open from Easter to October and the gardens all year round. Look out for events like concerts, storytelling and historic re-enactments on the premises.

Close to the entrance of Calke Abbey is the Tramway Bridge (also referred to as the Ticknall Arch bridge, or the Horseshoe bridge), a grade II listed structure. It was built in 1802 to link brickyards and limeyards to the Ashby canal at Willesley as it was too expensive to extend the canal to the north.

> Step back to life in Victorian times by visiting Calke Abbey

Calke Abbey

Reservoirs

Managed by
Severn Trent
Water, the two
main reservoirs
in this area offer
excellent
facilities for
boating, fishing
and hiking and
are home to very
active sailing
clubs.

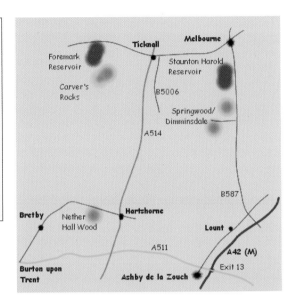

Directions

- Exit the A42 at junction 13 towards Ashby and at the roundabout towards Melbourne
- **Dimminsdale** and **Springwood** are to the left at the southern edge of **Staunton Harold Reservoir**
- Turn left towards the **Staunton Harold Reservoir Visitor Centre** just before Melbourne
- Take the road west through Ticknall to the **Foremark Reservoir** and **Carver's Rocks**
- Back to **Hartshorne** and turn right towards Bretby past the **Nether Hall Wood**
- At **Bretby** turn left towards the A511 and rejoin the A42 again at junction 13 from the A511.

STAUNTON HAROLD RESERVOIR

Staunton Harold Reservoir is a 84 ha (210 acre) reservoir and visitor centre built and managed by Severn Trent Water. It is home to the Staunton Harold sailing club, one of the largest and most active sailing clubs in the region and you can enjoy dinghy and sail boating with the club. The visitor centre has regular exhibitions, three dimensional displays and a very well equipped children's play area. Walks link the reservoir to Calke Abbey and the area is popular for fishing and bird watching around the lake and the wild flower meadow.

The play area and sailing at Staunton Harold Reservoir (above)

Walkway in Dimminsdale Wood (right)

Springwood and Dimminsdale are two nature reserves near the southern end of the Staunton Harold Reservoir. Dimminsdale is on the site of a disused limestone quarry and the name is said to have been derived from 'demon's dale' because of the glow of the kiln fires at night. A rockfall in one of the quarry tunnels around 1850 caused the quarry to be abandoned. The reserve offers woodland walks through the disused lime quarry and is especially attractive in spring when the ground is covered with snowdrops.

FOREMARK RESERVOIR

Foremark reservoir is a 92 ha (230 acre) nature reserve and reservoir of deep water with a lakeside lodge, managed by Severn Trent Water. It offers sailboat, dinghy and board sailing, and fishing, including facilities for disabled anglers. The lake is known for rainbow and brown trout fishing, catches averaging 1.5 kg (3.3 lb). The lake and nature reserve offer woodland walks, bird watching, picnic areas, a children's play area and information point.

Carver's Rocks just south of the reservoir, one of the largest disused stone quarries, is now a popular woodland managed by the Derbyshire Wildlife Trust. The rocky outcrops offer a popular climbing venue for top roping or solo rock climbing but should be treated with respect as a SSSI for geology and plants. Horseshoe Trail near Foremark is a 20 km (12.5 mile) figure of eight route for walking, horseriding and cycling.

Fishing at Foremark Reservoir

HARTSHORNE

The name apparently refers to the shape of the sandstone ridge next to the village, which was said, if viewed from a certain angle, looked like a stag's (or hart's) head. Another theory credits the name to a Hirschorn family who settled there from German Saxony around 300 AD. In the Domesday Book Hartshorne had two manors owned by Henry de Ferrers, and during the Civil War it sided with Ashby on the Royalist cause.

During the industrial revolution steel screws were manufactured at Hartshorne screw mill, today a popular restaurant and worth a visit. In the late 1700s and early 1800s small clay/pottery works started, using the white clay dug from the Wooden Box (now Woodville) area. Most of the potteries closed in the 1950s. Coal and ironstone were mined during the early 19th century.

Nether Hall Wood is a 8.5 ha (21 acre) mixed Woodland Trust wood between Hartshorne and Bretby with car parking facilities.

BRETBY

The name Bretby can be traced back to the Danish occupation, meaning 'the Place of the English'.

The village is reachable by leafy lanes. Stanhope Bretby was the site of Bretby Colliery, but has since been redeveloped into a business park housing, amongst others, the British Coal's research establishment.

There was a Bretby Castle, built as a fortified manor house in the 13th century and demolished in the 16th century for a Hall and enclosed park of 243 ha (600 acres). Only the Hall and lakes in this estate still exist. One of the owners of the estate was Lord Cameron, the Egyptologist, who sold the property to finance the famous expedition to search for the tomb of Tutankhamun with Howard Carter.

The present Hall is being redeveloped into private residential suites. The village green still features an old water pump.

Water pump in Bretby village

5 Rivers and Valleys

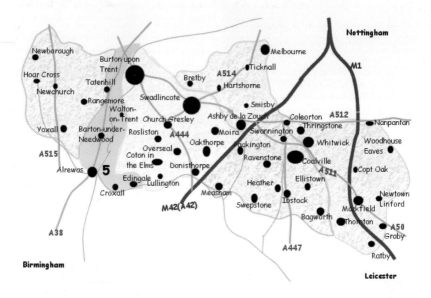

EXPLORE THE TRENT VALLEY IN TWO SECTIONS

- Burton upon Trent
- The Trent Valley (Barton-under-Needwood to Alrewas and back)

Rivers play a prominent part in the evolution and history of The National Forest. The River Trent flows through the western part of the Forest, forming the western border of the Midlands coalfields and the eastern border of the ancient Needwood Forest. As one of the major rivers in the Midlands it guided the ancient Salt Way between Chester and the South, becoming Ryknild Street (currently the A38), the only significant Roman road through the region. During the 19th century the Trent and Mersey Canal running between the A38 and the River Trent, was built to transport coal and other natural resources from the central coalfields.

The Mease forms the southern border of The National Forest and an old Salt Way went along its banks towards Leicester and the Charnwood Forest. Alrewas and Croxall, situated where the rivers Mease and Trent join with the River Tame from the south, form excellent sites for river woodlands and hide-outs for water birds and animals. Croxall Lakes is a sanctuary for otters under development near Croxall.

Information in Brief

Information Centres:

East Staffordshire Borough Council
Town Hall, King Edward Place, Burton upon Trent, Staffs DE14 2EB
Tel: 01283 508000
e-mail: tic@eaststaffsbc.gov.uk
Website: www.eaststaffsbc.gov.uk

Burton Tourist Information Centre
183 High Street, Burton upon Trent DE14 1HN
Tel: 01283 516609
e-mail: tic@eaststaffsbc.gov.uk
Website: www.lichfield.gov.uk
Moving to Bass Museum in September 2003

Lichfield Tourist Information Centre
Donegal House, Bore Street, Lichfield WS13 6NE
Tel: 01543 308209
e-mail: tic@lichfield-tourist.co.uk
Website: www.lichfield.gov.uk

Woodlands and Parks:

Alrewas: National Memorial Arboretum
Branston Water Park

Burton upon Trent: Trent Washlands, Stapenhill Gardens
Croxall: Wildlife haven
Wychnor: Wychnor Park

Canals, Lakes and Reservoirs:

Barton Turns Marina (moorings for boats)
Branston Water Park (boating, wind-surfing, fishing)
Rivers Mease and Tame (fishing, birdwatching)
River Trent (river boating, fishing)
Trent and Mersey Canal (canal boats)

Places of Interest:

Burton upon Trent: Brewhouse Art Centre, Bass Museum of Brewing, Ferrybridge, Meadowside and Shobnall Leisure Centres, Marstons Brewery tours, Shopping Centre and Market
Catton Hall
Wychnor Hall

Relevant Websites

www.burtonchoice.co.uk
www.canaljunction.co.uk
www.nationalforest.org

International memorial and Millennium Chapel for Peace and Forgiveness at the National Memorial

Arboretum, Alrewas

Burton upon Trent

Burton upon Trent is the largest town in The National Forest and was a river crossing from around 600. Its participation in various wars had devastating results, but it managed to recover and thrive on its industries of brewing, milling and trade along the river and the canal.

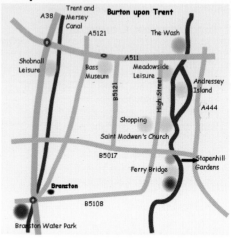

Directions

Burton upon Trent can be reached from
- The A38 at various exits, or
- From the A42 junction 13 and taking the A511 to the west
- From the M42 at junction 11 and the A444 west.

Ferry Bridge over River Trent with St Peter's Church in the background

BURTON UPON TRENT

Burton upon Trent dates back to around 653 when Saint Modwen and her nuns started a religious settlement on the island of Andressey in the River Trent where they became known for curing skin and eye ailments with water from the local well. This settlement was destroyed during the Danish invasion.

St Modwen's Church (above)
Abbey Inn (below)

Around 1002 Wulfric Spot, the Earl of Mercia and Chief Councillor of State for King Ethelread, founded a Benedictine Abbey and built a shrine to guard the remains of Saint Modwen on the banks of the River Trent. The town of Burton upon Trent developed around the Abbey and the current Abbey Inn contains parts of the infirmary of this Abbey. The Abbey was one of the few not destroyed by King Henry VIII in 1540, but gifted to Sir John Paget. The current manor hall, built in the late 1700s, is on the site of the original Abbey.

The parish church of St Modwen, off the High Street, is a fine example of Palladian type Gothic architecture. It was built in the 18th century on the site of the Saint's first settlement.

MILLING AND HOME OF BREWING

In the 13th century the monks of the Abbey were also instrumental in starting one of Burton's major industries when they discovered that the underground water in Burton is ideal for brewing. The brewing industry however only took off in the 18th century and by the late 1800s Burton upon Trent boasted 35 breweries. Only a few are still in existence, such as Coors (previously Bass), Marston's and Ind Coope Breweries. The Bass Museum of Brewing is a popular visitor attraction hosting exhibitions, a collection of vintage vehicles, the famous Coors Shire horses, a working Cooperage, Micro Brewery, gift shop, bar and restaurant facilities. Tours through the Marston's brewery can be arranged with the Brewery itself.

> Burton upon Trent also known as the home of brewing

Before the breweries, Burton was famous for its various mills for fulling, grinding flour and forging, mostly using water power from the River Trent. Robert Peel and William Yates were two of the industrialists building and using the mills during the 18th century. They

Swans at Ferry Bridge

constructed the Bond End canal to divert water from the Trent to the mills.

A ferry crossing over the Trent was operative from the 14th century for about 400 years after which it was replaced by bridges. The Ferry Bridge, gifted by Lord Burton to the town in 1889 is a unique suspension design with chains made from flat iron, riveted to the ends of the main girders. It is still very popular with visitors today.

Ferry trips are available on the 'Dingle Belle' from Ferry Bridge in the summer. Lord Burton also gave many fine buildings to the town, including the Town Hall, St Margaret's Church and St Paul's Church.

Burton upon Trent today is the largest town in The National Forest and offers excellent visitor attractions. The shopping facilities in the pedestrianised centre of town around High Street, are of top quality and include three covered centres, facilities for disabled shoppers, and an 800-year-old market, open on Thursdays, Fridays and Saturdays. The main Tourist Information Centre is in the High Street near the market (moving to the Bass Museum in 2003).

The Brewhouse Arts Centre is a multi-purpose building for theatre, galleries, cinema and bistro near the shopping area. It offers ongoing entertainment of theatre, live music, dance events and exhibitions throughout the year.

Stapenhill Gardens in Spring (above)

Statue of 'The Cooper' outside the Bass Museum (left)

(above) Weekend sport on Trent Washlands (above right) Model boat sailing on Branston Water Park

Burton upon Trent also offers excellent sporting and leisure facilities in the Shobnall Leisure Centre for sport and the Meadowside Leisure Centre for swimming, squash and an 18 hole golf course. The Trent Washlands was opened to the public in 1841 for sport and is today popular for walks, children's play areas, picnics, cycling and sport. The filled in Bond End canal and disused rail track have also been redeveloped as a walkway and cycle track. Stapenhill Gardens offer formal and informal flower displays, including an annual tulip festival. The Burton Festival during September is very popular, offering various events.

Pedestrian shopping street in Burton upon Trent

BRANSTON AND BRANSTON WATER PARK

Branston, the original home of Branston Pickle since the 1920s, is today nearly integrated with Burton upon Trent. The A38 through the village enabled an industrial centre to develop next to the road. Over the centuries the village had many owners including Eadwig, a Saxon Thane, Lady Godiva, Burton Abbey and eventually Sir William Paget and his descendants.

Branston Water Park is a 16 ha (40 acre) resort of woodland and lake behind the Branston industrial estate. The lake is popular for model boat sailing and fishing. The 1.6 km (1 mile) trail around the lake and woodland offers good opportunities for birdwatching.

> Branston, the original home of Branston Pickles and a popular Water Park.

The Trent Valley

The Trent valley is one of the few locations of potential pre-historic occupation. Barton-under-Needwood and Alrewas yielded relics from bronze age settlements, and Alrewas is also the meeting point of early Salt Roads and the Roman Ryknild Street, now the A38.

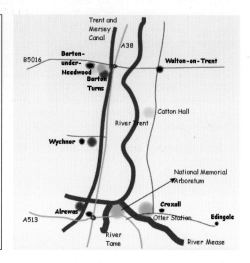

Directions

- Drive south from the A444 east of Burton upon Trent, along the eastern side of the river Trent along the picturesque narrow lanes to **Walton-on-Trent** and **Croxall. Catton Hall** is on the right between the villages
- Make a detour to **Edingale**
- From Croxall to **Alrewas** the new **Croxall Lakes** is on the right, followed by the **National Memorial Arboretum**
- From Alrewas drive north on the A38 and turn off to the left to **Wychnor** for canal sport
- Continue north and turn to **Barton-under-Needwood** and **Barton Turns Marina**
- Rejoin the A38 from Barton-under-Needwood.

WALTON-ON-TRENT

Walton-on-Trent is an ancient fording point of the River Trent, the place for instance where Edward II crossed the Trent in pursuit of Thomas, Earl of Lancaster and the disaffected barons. Nearby at Borough Hill Earthworks is a possible iron age fort, most likely the first settlement at Walton.

This eastern bank of the River Trent has always been popular for country residences. Halls built over the centuries include Drakelow Hall (now the site of the Drakelow Power Station), Walton Hall, Catton Hall and Croxall Hall.

Walton Hall is a private residence and a minor Georgian stately home built in 1723 on an older site. The de Ferrers of Walton owned the land from 1350 and sold it to William Taylor in 1680.

Catton Hall was owned by Henry de Ferrers during the time of the Domesday Book, but was acquired and remained in the hands of the current owners since 1405. Today it is a private home, open to the public on Monday afternoons during April to October.

In the Domesday Book the lord of the manor for Croxall was said to be Henry de Ferrers.

EDINGALE

Edingale is situated along the River Mease. Farms and the essential flood plains, restricted expansion of the village thereby making it a sought after residential area. At one time the centre of the village was at Croxall, but this moved back during the 17th century, including apparently the church bells! The main landowner used to be Henry de Ferrers.

Jos Holland from Edingale House Farm was a shire horse breeder of world acclaim. One of his champion horses, Edingale Mascot, was even exported to the USA for breeding.

CROXALL

Croxall is the point where three rivers meet: the Trent, Mease and Tame, and was first mentioned in 942 AD as part of a gift to Wulfsige the Black. It used to form a stopping point on the Salt Way before spliting into a route towards Tamworth and the route heading along both sides of the River Mease to the east.

Church in Edingale

The location of Croxall on the river bank made it profitable for sand and gravel workings. It is this 60 ha (150 acre) disused workings that was obtained for the National Forest Company, sponsored by Severn Trent Water, in September 2000.

The objective of this Croxall Lakes project is to develop a riverside wildlife haven as a 'service station' for otters and water voles. The final development will include otter holes (including log piles), shallows and reed cover, and selective fencing to ensure protected areas for resting otters.

The location is already good for bird watching, including a lake, meadow grassland and wetlands.

NATIONAL MEMORIAL ARBORETUM

Between Croxall and Alrewas, on the banks of the Trent, is the National Memorial Arboretum, 60 ha (150 acres) of new trees. It was created on the site of a disused gravel quarry as a memorial to the 80 million people who lost their lives in conflict during the 20th century.

A visit to the Arboretum is highly recommended for anyone who would like to remember family or friends lost in acts of war. Do not be deceived by the austere impression you get from the road. Once inside, you cannot help but be moved by the living forest memorial to the dead.

40,000 trees have been planted to date in a well constructed pattern of plots and groves dedicated to the Services, featuring the Golden Grove, the UN Spiral, a growing collection of sculptures and much more. Cuttings from a small-leafed lime tree, possibly the oldest in the country (possibly more than 6,000 years old), were used to create the Millennium Avenue. Individuals or groups may arrange to donate and plant trees in the forest.

Britain's only Millennium Chapel for Peace and Forgiveness is in the National Memorial Arboretum, in memory of the millions who lost their lives in conflict during the 20th century

Entrance to the National Memorial Arboretum (above)

Memorial Tree in the Golden ring, National Memorial Arboretum (left)

In the Millennium Chapel of the National Memorial Arboretum

The Arboretum also contains Britain's only Millennium Chapel of Peace and Forgiveness, and offers walks, picnic facilities, and dining at the Arbour restaurant.

ALREWAS

Relics were found around Alrewas of possible iron age occupation dating back to around 1200 BC. Alrewas was situated alongside early Salt Ways and it is possible that due to the flooding of the Trent and the Tame, the location was used as a stopping station, thus growing into the iron age village. Ryknild Street, the Roman Road (now the A38) also passes near Alrewas.

In 771 Alrewas was known as Allerwas from Aldr (alders) and waesse (marsh), aptly describing its situation between the two rivers. In the Domesday Book mention was made of eel fishing as a source of income.

The current village is picturesque with many 16 – 17th century thatched roofed, timber-framed cottages. The original road to Kings Bromley used to go along Mill Lane, which is now a dead end. In 1775 George Adams of Orgreave Hall apparently had the road closed to stop traffic passing his front door!

The Trent and Mersey Canal flows through Alrewas, making it a popular stopover for boaters. The Old Boat Inn (previously known as the Navigation Pub) is one of the stopover spots. The towpath along the canal is now a popular route for walking, and the banks of the canal for fishing.

Old Boat Inn on the Trent and Mersey canal at Alrewas (above)

Timber-framed cottage in Alrewas (right)

WYCHNOR

Wychnor is really a collection of farms with a church on the banks of the Trent and Mersey Canal, north of Alrewas. One of the popular annual events is a boat rally on the canal in August.

There is a story linked to Wychnor Hall that Sir Philip de Somerville was granted the manor by Edward III, on condition that he kept a flitch of bacon hanging in his hall as an offering to any couple who could prove that they were still happily married after one year and one day. Nobody apparently won the flitch! The Hall is today owned by a company for private member holidays.

BARTON TURNS MARINA

Barton Turns Marina on the Trent and Mersey Canal is a marina offering walks in the 26 ha (65 acre) newly planted forest. The Marina has over 320 berths for permanent and temporary moorings.

The Trent and Mersey Canal, opened in 1770, has recently been designated a conservation area with its number of hump-backed arched canal bridges and the Grade II listed 18th century three storey Wharf House at Barton Turns.

Arched bridge over Trent & Mersey Canal (above)

Barton Turns Marina

BARTON-UNDER-NEEDWOOD

The area around Barton-under-Needwood claims to have been inhabited since Neolithic times with evidence of:

- A timber version of Stonehenge at Catholme
- A bronze age (1500 BC) round barrow near Tuckholme
- Roman settlement south of Fatholme Lane east of the railway line
- An Anglo-Saxon settlement gifted to Wulfsige the Black in 942
- A Danish settlement gifted to Henry de Ferrers by William the Conqueror.

The name Barton comes from the Saxon 'Bretone' meaning grain fields, barley store or rickyard, demonstrating the agricultural nature of the village. Over the years it managed to retain its character in spite of the developments brought by the canal and railways.

Around 1480 triplet boys were born to William Taylor (a game warden in the Forest of Needwood) and his wife Joan. So unusual was this event and the fact that the boys grew up to adulthood, that Henry VII funded their education up to university level 'beyond the seas' –

possibly France or Italy. The first-born, John, Doctor of Decrees, went on to occupy influential positions in Henry's offices, the peak of which was Master of the Rolls (1527) and archdeacon of Halifax (1528). The latter position he had to surrender because of a diseased leg and he died in 1534. His generous gifts to Barton included the St James Church supposedly near his parent's home. The inscriptions over alternate pillars of the nave of this church tell of his illustrious career, and between them is the coat of arms adopted by him, depicting the triplets. The Church is a Grade II listed building as a rare example of a church which was completed within one lifetime. The John Taylor High School built in 1957 was named after him.

Another interesting family in the village were the Hollands who lived there for more than 600 years. Richard Holland was granted rights and privileges in the Forest of Needwood in 1314 by the Earl of Lancaster, and since then members of the family took part in the various battles around the village, were church wardens, charity trustees and overseers of the poor (16th to 17th centuries). John Holland (1798 to 1876) became the first village postmaster, succeeded by his daughter and granddaughter. Miss Mary Holland, the last of the Hollands in Barton-under-Needwood was a suffragette in the early 1900s and governor at the Thomas Russell school from 1880. In 1923 she was made Justice of Peace for the County of Stafford, a position she held until her death in 1959.

St James' Church in Barton-under-Needwood

6 Needwood Forest

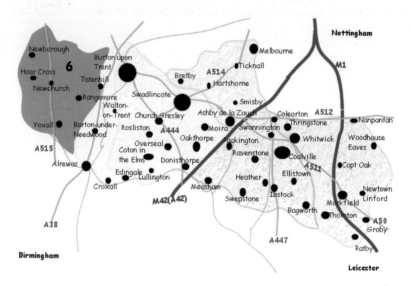

EXPLORE THE NEEDWOOD FOREST
AS A SINGLE ENTITY

Needwood was originally classed as a chase with woodlands and open meadows. As an ancient hunting forest or chase, it was held by the Duchy of Lancaster until the accession of Henry IV, when it became the possession of the Crown. Agardsley (later Newborough) was the only Needwood settlement mentioned in the Domesday Book.

Before enclosure only the hunting lodges of Byrkley, Ealand, Yoxall and Sherholt were in the forest. The Enclosures Act of 1803 however enabled Needwood Forest to be subdivided into the eight ancient parks of Agardsley, Stockley, Barton, Heynlyns, Sherholt, Castle Hay, Hanbury and Rolleston. The forest was slowly being destroyed by farming.

One peculiarity in Needwood Forest is that roads are in straight lines as if drawn with the assistance of a ruler. The Six Roads End in the north western corner of The National Forest is a good example of this phenomenon.

Small woodland parks and coppices are all that remain of the ancient Needwood Forest and mainly on private property, accessible only via public footpaths. The largest parks are Greaves Wood in the Northwest and the parks west of Newchurch, i.e. Braken Hurst Wood and Jackson's Bank.

Information in Brief

Information Centres:

East Staffordshire Borough
Council
Town Hall, King Edward Place
Burton upon Trent, Staffs
DE14 2EB
Tel: 01283 508000
e-mail: tic@eaststaffsbc.gov.uk
Website: www.eaststaffsbc.gov.uk

Burton Tourist
Information Centre
183 High Street, Burton upon
Trent DE14 1HN
Telephone: 01283 516609
e-mail: tic@eaststaffsbc.gov.uk
Website: www.eaststaffsbc.gov.uk
Moving to Bass Museum in
September 2003

Woodlands and Parks:

Greaves Wood
Newchurch: Jackson's Bank,
Braken Hurst Wood
Rangemore: Byrkley Park
Tatenhill: Battlestead Hill

Places of Interest:

Hoar Cross: Church of the Holy
Angels, Needwood Gliding club
Newborough: Piano Workshop
Newchurch: Tatenhill Airfield
Rangemore: Byrkley Park
Garden Centre

Relevant Websites:

www.sbap.org.uk
Natural areas around
Staffordshire
www.flyingzone.co.uk
www.nationalforest.org.co.uk

Jackson's Bank forest walk in the Duchy of Lancaster

Needwood

Only Newborough (then called Agardsley) was mentioned in the Domesday Book as a settlement in Needwood Forest . As a Royal Chase the forest was left undivided until the Enclosures Act of 1803.

Note the straight lines of the roads unlike other parts of The National Forest where older roads wind their way through the countryside.

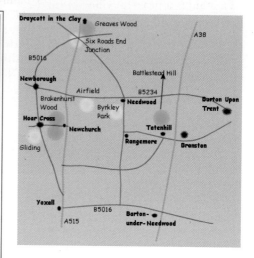

Directions

- Exit the A38 towards **Tatenhill**. **Battlestead Hill park** is to the right
- Drive west towards **Rangemore**, Rangemore Hall and **Byrkley Park**
- At Rangemore turn right towards Tutbury until the roundabout at **Needwood**. Take a detour to the **old war aerodrome** and Tatenhill Airfield to the west
- From Needwood travel northwest on the B5107 (Uttoxeter road) to **Six Roads End.** For **Greaves Wood**, turn right at Six Roads End (towards Hanbury) and take the left turn into Greaves Lane towards Draycott-in-the-Clay, then back to Six Roads End
- At Six Roads End take the turnoff for **Newborough** and continue towards **Hoar Cross**
- Turn right towards **Newchurch**, visiting **Braken Hurst Wood** and **Jackson's Bank** on the way
- At the cross roads, turn right towards **Yoxall**
- Drive through **Barton-under-Needwood** to rejoin the A38

TATENHILL

Tatenhill is a peaceful village with winding streets and attractive old houses. Battlestead Hill at Tatenhill is a 2.5 ha (6 acre) broadleaved Woodland Trust development with limited parking and good views.

New woodlands being created on Battlestead Hill

RANGEMORE

Like most of the villages in and around Needwood Forest, Rangemore is dominated by farming and horticulture, in addition to being a commuter residential area. Although the village only dates back to the early 19th century, Ravensmoor (which gave its name to the village) is on one of the former Salt Ways, the Aleswardesley. The village developed around Tatenhill Gate – one of the entrances to the Needwood Forest.

The village was constructed by order of Michael Thomas Bass who at that stage lived at the Rangemore House (later Hall) and built the cottages for his employees. The Bass family also built the church and later the Rangemore Club and Reading room for the villagers. Through the Bass family many famous persons visited the village and Hall which used to house a collection of fine art. Edward VII was one of these visitors.

Near the church in Rangemore is a group of tall Wellingtonia trees (known in California as *Sequoia Giganteum)* growing to 91 m (300 ft) high.

The Byrkley Park Garden Centre is a gardener's eden situated in the heart of the Needwood Forest. The centre offers everything not only for the keen gardener, but also for the whole family, including a play area, farm animals, tropical and cold water fish and a restaurant. The Centre occupies the walled garden of Byrkley Lodge, on the estate of Sir William Bass, and all areas are accessible for disabled users.

During World War II part of the Byrkley estate between Needwood and Newchurch, was used to build a wartime aerodrome, now used by local flying clubs/schools, including the East Staffordshire Flying Club and Tatenhill Aviation.

Farm animal centre at Byrkley Park Garden Centre

SIX ROADS END AND GREAVES WOOD

Six Roads End is the crossing point of three roads through Needwood Forest at the north western border of The National Forest. Unlike the traditional roads which follow the winding route of ancient tracks, the roads in the Needwood Forest seem to have been drawn with the assistance of a ruler! The A515 for instance has only one kink where the road passes Rangemore Hall.

Sign at Six Roads End with Greaves Wood in the background

Greaves Wood included in The National Forest, is only the eastern tip of a larger ancient forest in Marchington and Draycott. It offers well marked forest walks, with parking in lay-byes. Evidence of Celtic occupation of this part of the forest was found in Greaves Wood north of Six Roads End in the middle of the 19th century. The 'Needwood Torque' as it was dubbed is on permanent loan to the Romano-British Department of the British Museum in London.

NEWBOROUGH

The name of the village reflects the changes in the village history over the centuries. Originally known as Edgarslege (the pasture of Edgar the Saxon), it was changed to Agardsley after the Norman conquest. In the 12th century it became the New Borough of Agardsley by the new owners, the de Ferrers, but the latter part of the name was dropped as the village was given to Edmund, Duke of Lancaster after the de Ferrers fell out with the King. It is still in the Duchy of Lancaster. Agardsley was the only place in Needwood mentioned in the Domesday Book.

Sir Arthur Sullivan inaugurated the organ of the All Saints Church early in the 20th century. On Spring bank holiday the village holds a well dressing ceremony whereby the local wells and church are decorated with flowers and blessed, followed by a fun fair.

Newborough also offers an opportunity to visit a unique 'Piano Workshop', open on Wednesdays, Thursdays and Saturdays. where you are welcome to play or examine any of the instruments and see pianos being restored.

Bagot's Park near Newborough was famous for the Bagot goats presented to Sir John Bagot by Richard II.

Old Piano Workshop in Newborough

Church of the Holy Angels, Hoar Cross

HOAR CROSS

Hoar Cross is more a collection of houses rather than a structured village. Up to the middle of the 20th century just about all the villagers worked on the nearby Meynell estate, but like other local villages, it has become a commuter residential area since then.

The Church of the Holy Angels built in the Gothic style during the 19th century, was introduced to travellers by John Betjeman as the masterpiece of the architect, Bodley. A visitor's book shows that today it still attracts many visitors from all over the world. The unique Stages of the Cross are especially worth observing.

Other places of interest include the old water mill at Woodmill, possibly one of the oldest in Staffordshire, and the Spion Kop wood on the farm Ladysmith. Both the names of the wood and the farm were given to commemorate one of the Boer war battles in South Africa in the beginning of the 20th century! Woodmill also contains a short stretch of road which becomes a toad crossing area each February, to allow toads to reach a spawning pond.

Hoar Cross Hall is today a stately home health spa. The building is a grade II listed building, built by Sir Hugo Meynell for his wife Emily, the daughter of Viscount Halifax, and later rebuilt by Lord Scarsdale as a hunting lodge. The current hall offers hydrotherapy spa, pool and various sporting facilities including walks, golf, gym, tennis and boules.

A group of Woodlands between Hoar Cross and Newchurch include Braken Hurst Wood and Jackson's Bank. Jackson's Bank is a 32 ha (80 acres) mature mixed broadleaved and coniferous woodland open to the public by courtesy of the Duchy of Lancaster. It offers car parking, well marked trails and hard roadway for all-abilities walks but with steep hills. The Needwood Forest Gliding Club situated outside Hoar Cross is popular for regular and one-off gliding.

Jackson's Bank

NEWCHURCH

Newchurch used to be part of the ancient Needwood forest, a popular hunting ground for the Kings of England, and a custom still kept alive with the annual Meynell Hunt. Today it is an ecclesiastical parish servicing a few farms and houses from the church, built during the reign of George III. The Royal Coat of Arms still hangs in the church as a link to the past. The parish of Newchurch borders on the Duchy of Lancaster.

The two main hunting lodges within the Newchurch parish are Yoxall Lodge and Byrkley Lodge. Yoxall lodge was once the residence of Rev Thomas Gisborne known as a divine and poet and has since been rebuilt into a farm-house. Byrkley Lodge was the residence of the Bass family until it was pulled down in 1952.

YOXALL

The most widely accepted Saxon origin of the name Yoxall splits the word into 'Yox' (from yoke and oxen) and 'all' (from halgh meaning hidden place). The latter part is very suitable to this ancient market village hidden in the valley of the Swarbourn River near the south western border of the Needwood Forest.

Yoxall retained its agricultural self-contained character. Many families remained in Yoxall, and rectors, school-masters and doctors tended to stay for long periods. One of the old houses, the village shop of Tom Paget, can now be seen in the Staffordshire County Museum in Shugborough. It was dismantled and re-assembled in the museum as a typical village shop!

Today Yoxall is popular as a commuter residential area for Burton upon Trent, Lichfield and Birmingham, and offers active clubs in the village as well as good hiking and cycling trails. The Swarbourn river bank is also a good site for birdwatching.

Spring on the banks of the Swarbourn

Activities

In addition to the expected walks through the woods and parks in The National Forest, the region offers a rich selection of activities to choose from. Whether your preference is for hiking, action sport, history or shopping, this section provides a quick reference to help you plan your activities.

CATEGORIES OF ACTIVITIES

- Towns and villages (walks, shopping, museums, activity centres)
- Historical buildings and ruins
- Woodlands and Parks (hiking, all-abilities walks, bird-watching)
- Action Sport (water sport, horse riding, cycling, skiing, rock climbing, gliding, golf)

Information on opening hours, entrance charges and features change regularly. Contact the addresses, telephone numbers or websites listed in the Contacts Section for up-to-date information. Note that opening dates should be all year round unless otherwise stated, times will vary and should be checked on the websites or with the Tourist Information Centres.

Websites and contact information is in the final section of the book.

Towns and Villages

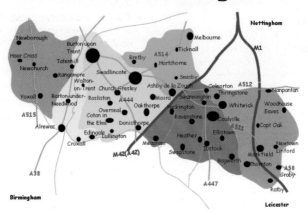

Alrewas

A picturesque village with 16th to 17th century thatched houses in traditional timber frames. The Trent and Mersey Canal flows through the village and the Old Boat Inn on the canal is a popular stopover for boaters.

Ashby de la Zouch

Follow the Ashby de la Zouch Heritage Trail and visit amongst others:
- Ashby de la Zouch Castle ruins, an English Heritage site with strong links to the Civil War, and featured in Sir Walter Scott's novel, *Ivanhoe*. Open all year at differing hours
- Ashby Museum with permanent displays of the town's rich history, open from Easter to September
- Experience the memories of Ashby, the Historic Spa Town of the Victorian era in the Royal Hotel, the period shops in Mill Lane Mews off North Street, or the shops and Market in Market Street

Barton-under-Needwood

Visit St James Church with the inscriptions and arms of John Taylor, the most famous of the triplets born in Barton-under-Needwood 1480. Visit Barton Turns Marina for mooring, walks and bird-watching.

Burton upon Trent

Burton upon Trent is the largest town in The National Forest and has much to offer the visitor:
- Visit the Bass Museum of Brewing or join a tour through the Marston's Brewery
- Watch local or visiting theatre and musical performances in the Brewhouse Arts Centre
- Keep fit at the Meadowside and Shobnall Leisure Centres
- Join a boat trip from Ferry Bridge on the Dingle Belle down the River Trent in summer
- Go shopping in the excellent pedestrianised and under-roof shopping centres and markets
- Go for walks on the Trent Washlands, and Andressey Island's sculpture trail, or Stapenhill Gardens

Coalville

Follow the Coalville Heritage Trail and experience:
- The Clocktower surrounded by historic public houses from the mining era
- The Belvoir pedestrian shopping centre, market and shops along Belvoir Road

- Snibston Discovery Park on the site of Snibston Number 2 Colliery.

Coleorton
A village created and sculptured by surface mining since medieval times. Visit Coleorton Wood on the site of a disused mine and experience the unique characteristics of this village and its surrounding hamlets.

Groby
Thriving village on the edge of Charnwood Forest and historically the home of the Beaumonts, de Ferrers and Greys in Groby Old Hall. Picnic at Groby Pool.

Hoar Cross
To the west of the Needwood Forest. The Holy Angels Church is known for its excellent architecture. Hoar Cross Hall is today an exclusive stately home health spa.

Markfield
The highest and coldest village in Leicestershire. Visit the site of the disused Markfield quarry and picnic at the Altar Stones or Blacksmith's Field.

Measham
The museum in Measham is open on Tuesdays and Saturday mornings and contains historical artefacts from the village including Rockingham-ware terra cotta pottery. Many of the older houses in High Street still show the larger size 'jumbricks' made in Measham to reduce taxation during the 18th/19th centuries.

Melbourne
A walk through Melbourne covers sites like:
- Melbourne Hall and its lake, once home to William Lamb, 2nd Viscount of Melbourne and Prime Minister. Walks around the pool and cast iron 'birdcage' are recommended (open during summer)
- The Church of St Michael and St Mary, also referred to as a cathedral in miniature
- The Thomas Cook Memorial cottages built by the travel entrepreneur

Thomas Cook who was born in Melbourne
- The Leisure Centre, a popular indoor leisure centre and swimming pool.

Moira
At the heart of The National Forest. Visit Conkers for hands-on experience and discovery. Don't forget the Moira Furnace on the banks of the redeveloped Ashby Canal.

Nanpantan
Nanpantan, on the edge of The National Forest, offers some outdoor activities for visitors:
- Nanpantan Reservoir offers good fishing facilities
- Home Farm is an organic farm between Nanpantan and Woodhouse Eaves for walks, play area and shops.

Newborough
In the Needwood Forest. A well dressing ceremony is held on Spring bank holiday. Visit the Piano Workshop on Wednesdays, Thursdays and Saturdays.

Newtown Linford
A typical forest village with thatched cottages and attractive cricket field in Charnwood. The entrance to Bradgate Park/House is in the town.

Packington
Watch out for the roundhouse or village lockup, one of the 200 remaining in the country.

Ratby
View the remnants of an iron age settlement at Ratby Burroughs or wander through the Martinshaw and Peartree Woods on the outskirts of the village.

Smisby
Smisby has one of the 200 remaining roundhouses or village lockups in the country.
   The Bluebell Arboretum and Nursery offers rare trees, shrubs and plants on display or for sale.

Swadlincote

Swadlincote is a busy town offering much for the active tourist, such as:

- Green Bank Leisure Centre for swimming, squash and fitness
- The Swadlincote Ski Centre for dry slope skiing and tobogganing
- Swadlincote Woodland park opposite the Ski Centre for walks and children's play area
- Jungle Madness, an indoor soft play centre for the youngsters
- Pedestrianised shopping area offering a wide variety of shops including markets
- Two potteries, Sharpe's Pottery dating back to the early 19th century and TG Green famous for its blue and white striped Cornish Ware.

Swannington

A winding village on the A447. The Swannington Heritage Trail takes you through the village and the railway incline, built for the first commercial railway in the UK. Visit Hough Mill and the Gorse Field.

Swithland and Woodhouse Eaves

Picturesque Charnwood Forest villages featuring houses from local rock (Markfield) and Swithland roof-tiles.

Ticknall

Contains one of the few roundhouses or village lockups still in the country. Also the iron water standpipes erected by Sir Vauncey Harpur Crewe for the villagers in 1914. Visit the nearby Calke Abbey and Tramway bridge.

Thornton

The Thornton Reservoir at the edge of the village offers an excellent day out for the whole family for walks or fishing.

Whitwick and Thringstone

Relax in Whitwick's modern Hermitage Leisure Centre in Silver Street. Outdoor facilities include bowls and the 18-hole Hermitage Lakeside golf course. The Rt Hon. Charles Booth is buried in the churchyard of Saint Andrew's church in Thringstone.

Historical Buildings and Ruins

Ashby Castle Ruins, Ashby de la Zouch

Built in the 12th century the castle played an active role in the Civil War and featured in Sir Walter Scott's novel *Ivanhoe*. Open daily during the summer and selectively in winter.

Bradgate House, Newtown Linford

Birthplace of Lady Jane Grey, the nine day Queen of England in 1553. Museum open March to November.

Byrkley Park Garden Centre, Rangemore

Garden Centre, playground and farm animal centre in the walled garden of the old Byrkley Lodge.

Calke Abbey, Ticknall

Baroque mansion house, frozen in time since the Victorian era and filled with collections made by the owners over the centuries. Open Easter to October.

Donington le Heath Manor House, Coalville

Manor house built around 1280 and restored as a 17th century period house.

Grace Dieu Abbey Ruins, Thringstone

Ruins of one of only two medieval nunneries in Leicestershire founded around 1235. Gifted to John Beaumont by Henry VIII after its dissolution.

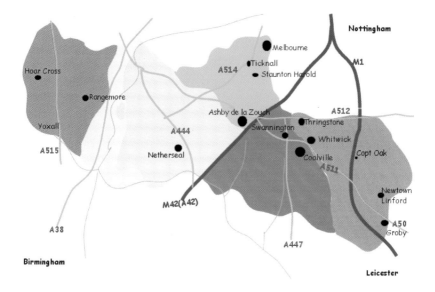

Grangewood Garden Centre, Netherseal

Grangewood Garden Centre is in the walled garden of Grangewood Hall.

Hough Mill, Swannington

A restored 18th century mill tower, with mill stones and artefacts. Open on Sundays and Saturday mornings from Easter to September.

Melbourne Hall and Park, Melbourne

Manor house dating back to the early 17th century and still in private ownership. Iron pergola in the garden casted by Robert Bakewell is also known as the Birdcage. The Hall is open on Tuesdays to Saturdays during August and the garden from April to September.

Moira Furnace

Furnace built on the banks of the Ashby Canal in 1804 and preserved as a museum.

Mount St Bernard Abbey, Whitwick

The first Catholic Abbey built in the country after the Reformation. Building started in 1835 but only consecrated after World War II. Active monastery, open to casual visitors and residents as a retreat.

Snibston Discovery Park, Coalville

Snibston Number 2 Colliery was preserved for the nation and developed into an excellent living museum and activity centre.

Staunton Harold Church and Ferrers Centre for Arts and Crafts

The first house was built in 1324 by Sir William de Staunton and it remained in the de Ferrers family until it was sold in 1954. The church is a National Trust building open all year round. The Ferrers Centre for Arts and Crafts is in the Georgian courtyard next to the house with a gallery shops and workshops.

Ulverscroft Abbey Ruins, Copt Oak

Founded in the 11th century by Robert de Bossu, it was an active abbey ministering to the poor until its dissolution by Henry VIII. Today only a ruin remains on private property.

101

Woodlands and Parks

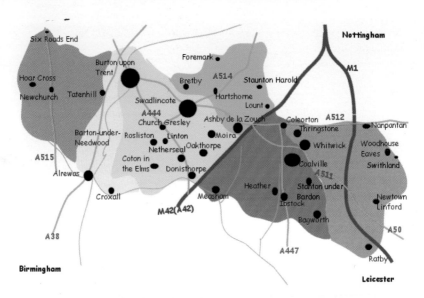

Alrewas, National Memorial Arboretum (all-abilities)
A newly planted war memorial forest with the only Millennium Chapel in the country. Walks and picnic facilities.

Bagworth (all-abilities)
Bagworth Heath Wood – New woodland on disused colliery with all-abilities walking trails.

Centenary Wood, Royal Tigers Wood, managed by the Woodland Trust with good walks.

Bretby, Nether Hall Wood
Established Woodland Trust development with hikes.

Burton upon Trent (all-abilities)
Trent Washlands - Walks on all-ability and sculpture trails. Stapenhill Gardens - Formal and informal floral displays and tulip festival in spring.

Church Gresley, Swainspark Wood
Redeveloped woodland park at the edge of an active mine on reclaimed land.

Coalville, Bardon Hill
Footpath only to the top of the highest hill in Leicestershire from Copt Oak.

Coleorton, Coleorton Wood
Woodland on disused colliery with mown paths and signs.

Coton in the Elms, Coton Wood
Mainly broadleaf woods and grasslands with good views.

Croxall, Croxall Lakes
Haven for otters and other water animals on the River Mease (under development).

Donisthorpe/Oakthorpe (all-abilities)
New Wood, Woodland Park, Saltersford Valley Picnic Area, Willesley Wood. Woods around Donisthorpe and Oakthorpe developed on reclaimed land and disused collieries. Oakthorpe, Willesley and Saltersford Woods have all-ability trails.

Foremark, Carver's Rocks
Woodland walks around and near the reservoir developed by the Wildlife Trust.

Six Roads End, Greaves Wood
Ancient forest near Six Roads End with walks.

Ibstock, Sence Valley Forest Park (all-abilities)
New broadleaved and conifer plantation with lakes, on a disused colliery.

Linton
Woodland Trust developments of Long Close, Top Wood and Foxley Wood. Mainly broadleaved woodlands with local information board and walks.

Lount, Lount Nature Reserve
Managed by Leicestershire Council and Rutland Wildlife Trust as a mature woodland reserve with grassland and ponds.

Moira (all-abilities)
Conkers - woodland, walks and outdoor action trail next to the restored Ashby canal.
Sarah's Wood, a transformed woodland specially designed for children with special needs.

Nanpantan, Jubilee Wood, Outwoods
Woods presented to Leicestershire County Council to commemorate the Queen's Silver Jubilee. Walks, especially in spring when the woods are covered with bluebells.

Netherseal
Grangewood is a private woodland on reclaimed land with ponds and walks. Grangewood Zoo is home to tropical brids and animals.

Newchurch (all-abilities)
Braken Hurst Wood and Jackson's Bank, mature broadleaved and mixed conifer woods. Jackson's Bank has hard surfaced paths for all-abilities trails but the hills are steep.

Newtown Linford, Bradgate Park (all-abilities)
Bradgate park is popular for walks, riding and cycling.

Ratby (all-abilities)
Martinshaw Wood, Peartree and Burroughs woods are Woodland Trust properties of broadleaved and conifer trees and good walking trails.

Rosliston, Rosliston Forestry Centre (all-abilities)
The Forestry Centre was developed by South Derbyshire District Council as a mixed broadleaf, and conifer plantation with excellent walks, bird hide and activities for children.

Stanton under Bardon, Billa Barra
Woodland developed on a disused quarry site. Walks and information boards on site.

Staunton Harold
Walks in established Springwood and Dimminsdale.

Swadlincote (all-abilities)
Swadlincote Woodland Park, newly planted woodland park with excellent paths and views. Children's play area available.

Swithland, Swithland Wood
An ancient wood in Charnwood Forest with walks, horse trails and cycle trails. Popular for walks.

Tatenhill, Battlestead Hill
Woodland Trust and private woodland developments on Battlestead Hill

Thringstone, Grace Dieu Wood (all-abilities)
Part of the Grace Dieu estate including the ruins of a medieval priory. Good cycle trail was built as part of the millennium developments.

Woodhouse Eaves, Beacon Hill
Established woodland at lower part of Beacon hill and walks on the hill.

BIRD WATCHING

Check the general websites, including:
www.birdinguk.co.uk

Action Sport

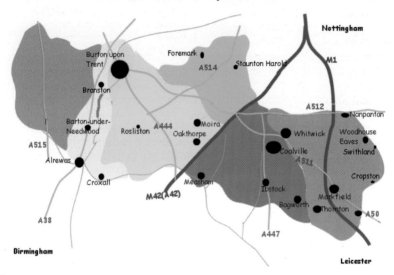

WATER SPORT

General Websites and Clubs:
www.go-fish.co.uk
www.canalsjunction.co.uk
www.shsc.org.uk (Staunton Harold
Sailing Club)
www.luec.freeserve.co.uk (Leics
Underwater Exploration Club)

Alrewas
Fishing along the Trent and Mersey
Canal. Popular stopover for longboats on
the Trent and Mersey Canal.

Bagworth Heath Wood
Fishing on the lake in the Wood.

Barton Turns Marina
The Marina offers 320 berths for
permanent and temporary mooring off
the Trent and Mersey Canal.

Branston Water Park
Model boat sailing and fishing on the
lake.

Burton upon Trent
Cruise on the *Dingle Belle* from Ferry
Bridge along the river Trent.

Coalville, Whitwick
Fishing at the Hermitage and Snibston
lakes.

Cropston Reservoir
Reservoir under management of Severn
Trent Water. Fishing.

Foremark Reservoir
Managed by Severn Trent Water. Known
for rainbow and brown trout fishing.
Sailing and dinghy sailing club.

Ibstock, Sence River
Forest Park
Fishing allowed at one of the lakes in
the park.

Moira, Ashby Canal
Narrowboat sailing between Moira
Furnace and Conkers. Canal is being
restored to its full original length.

Nanpantan Reservoir
Man-made lake with easy access around
the lake. Known for carp, bream, small
perch and roach.

**Oakthorpe,
Willesley Wood Lake**
Man-made lake following subsidence. Shallow edges and popular for carp. Tickets bought on the banks.

Rosliston, Beehive Farm
Facilities for disabled fishing. Permits required from the farm.

Staunton Harold Reservoir
Manged by Severn Trent Water. Fishing and sailing. Home of Staunton Harold Sailing Club.

Swithland Quarry
Disused slate quarry with deep water to 50 m (164 ft). Used to practise deep cold water diving. Diving only for the experienced and through the club.

Thornton Nature Reservoir
Managed by Severn Trent Water. Known for trout fishing. Easy access around the lake.

HORSE RIDING

Check general websites:
www.pcuk.org (The Pony Club, UK)
www.nationalforest.org

Parks especially suitable for horse-riding include:
Beehive Farm, Rosliston
Bradgate Park, Newtown Linford
Broombriggs Farm, Woodhouse Eaves
Grangewood Farm, Netherseal
Knowleshill Equestrian Centre, Ticknall
Markfield Pony Club
Swithland Wood, Swithland
West Beacon Field, Beacon Hill
Sence Valley Forest Park, Ibstock
Rosliston Forestry Centre

CYCLING

Check general websites:
www.nationalforest.org

In additional to cycle tracks promoted on The National Forest website, the following parks are especially suitable for cycling.
Bradgate Park, Newtown Linford
Donisthorpe Woodland Park
Rosliston Forestry Centre
Sence Valley Forest Park
Swithland Wood, Swithland

TEAM SPORT

All larger towns and most villages have team sport facilities. Check on the local or regional websites for more information.

SKIING

Swadlincote
Dry ski slope offering all-weather nursery slope, 160m (175 yd) main run and 650 m (710 yd) toboggan run with club house and restaurant.
www.skihoo.co.uk

ROCK CLIMBING

Climbing opportunities exist at most disused and current quarry sites. Check the website for information:
www.leicesterclimbs.f9.co.uk

GLIDING/ FLYING

Newchurch and Hoar Cross
The World War II aerodrome near Newchurch is used by local clubs such as the East Staffordshire Flying Club and Tatenhill Aviation. The Needwood Forest Gliding Club is at Hoar Cross.
www.flyingzone.co.uk
www.gogliding.co.uk

GOLF

Private and municipal golf clubs and courses are available at most towns and villages. Check the relevant websites for more information.
www.nwleics.gov.uk
www.south-derbys.gov.uk
www.eaststaffsbc.gov.uk
www.uk-golfguide.com

Key Contacts

COUNCILS

Leicestershire County Council

Tourism Section, County Hall, Glenfield, Leics LE3 8RJ
Tel: 0116 265 7039
e-mail: tourism@leicestershire.gov.uk
Website: www.leics.gov.uk

North West Leicestershire District Council

Council Offices
Stenson Road, Coalville, Leics LE67 3FJ
Tel: 01530 454545
e-mail: regeneration@nwleicestershire.gov.uk
Website: www.nwleics.gov.uk

East Staffordshire Borough Council

Town Hall, King Edward Place, Burton upon Trent, Staffs DE14 2EB
Tel: 01283 508000
e-mail: tic@eaststaffsbc.gov.uk
Website: www.eaststaffsbc.gov.uk

South Derbyshire District Council

Civic Offices, Civic Way, Swadlincote, Derbys. DE11 0AH
Tel: 01283 595754
e-mail: tourism@south-derbys.gov.uk
Website: www.south-derbys.gov.uk

TOURIST INFORMATION CENTRES

Coalville Tourist Information Centre

Snibston Discovery Park, Ashby Road, Coalville LE67 3LN
Tel: 01530 813608
e-mail: coalville.tic@nwleicestershire.gov.uk
Website: www.nwleics.gov.uk

Conkers

Rawdon Road, Moira, Derbys DE12 6GA
Tel: 01283 216633
e-mail: info@visitconkers.com
Website: www.visitconkers.com

Ashby de la Zouch Tourist Information Centre

North Street, Ashby de la Zouch LE65 1HU
Tel: 01530 411767
e-mail: ashby.tic@nwleicestershire.gov.uk
Website: www.nwleics.gov.uk

Burton Tourist Information Centre

183 High Street, Burton upon Trent DE14 1HN
Tel: 01283 516609
e-mail: tic@eaststaffsbc.gov.uk
Website: www.eaststaffsbc.gov.uk
Moving to Bass Museum in September 2003

Loughborough Tourist Information Centre

Town Hall, Market Place, Loughborough, LE11 3EB
Tel: 01509 218113
Website: www.charnwoodbc.gov.uk

Lichfield Tourist Information Centre

Donegal House, Bore Street, Lichfield WE13 6NE
Tel: 01543 308209
e-mail: tic@lichfield-tourist.co.uk
Website: www.lichfield.gov.uk

Swadlincote Tourist Information Centre

Civic Way, Swadlincote, Derbys. DE11 0AH
Tel: 01283 595739
e-mail: tourism@south-derbys.gov.uk
Website: www.south-derbys.gov.uk

Severn Trent Water

Website: www.stwater.co.uk
Tel: Individual site numbers available
on the website.

ENVIRONMENTAL TRUSTS

The National Forest Company

Bath Lane, Moira, Swadlincote,
Derbyshire, DE12 6BD
Tel: 01283 551211
e-mail: discover@nationalforest.org
Website: www.nationalforest.org

British Trust for Conservation

Volunteers, Moira
Tel: 01283 2229096
Website: www.btcv.org

Forestry Commission

Great Eastern House, Tenison Road,
Cambridge CB1 2DU
Tel: 01223 314546
e-mail: enquiries@forestry.gsi.gov.uk
Website: www.forestry.gov.uk

National Trust

36 Queen Anne's Gate, London SW1H 9AS
Tel: 0870 6095380
e-mail: enquiries@thenationaltrust.org.uk
Website: www.nationaltrust.org.uk

Woodland Trust

Autumn Park, Grantham, Lincolnshire
NG31 6LL
Tel: 01476 581111
e-mail: enquires@woodland-trust.org.uk
Website: www.woodland-trust.org.uk

Wildlife Trust

e-mail: info@wildlife-trust.cix.co.uk
Website: www.wildlifetrust.org.uk
Tel: Individual region numbers available
on the website.

TOWN/VILLAGE WEBSITES

www.anyvillage.co.uk
www.applebymagna.org.uk

www.barton-under-needwood.org.uk
www.burton2000.co.uk
www.burtonchoice.co.uk
www.charnwoodbc.gov.uk
www.hartshorne.org.uk
www.markfieldhistory.com
www.meashamparish.co.uk
www.melbourne-uk.com
www.smisby.org.uk
www.swannington-heritage.co.uk
www.willesleywood.co.uk
www.woodhouse-eaves.co.uk

TRAVEL

www.aboutbritain.com
www.countryside.gov.uk
Countryside character initiatives
www.english-nature.org.uk
www.information-britain.co.uk
www.theheritagetrail.co.uk
www.streetmap.co.uk

ACCOMMODATION

www.accomodata.co.uk
www.midlandspubs.co.uk
www.yha.org.uk
Youth Hostels England and Wales
Also check council websites

ACTIVITY WEBSITES

www.birdinguk.co.uk
www.canaljunction.com
www.carplakes.com
www.flyingzone.co.uk
www.go-fish.co.uk
www.healthfarms-uk.co.uk
www.leicesterclimbs.f9.co.uk
www.luec.freeserve.co.uk
Leicestershire Underwater Exploration Club
www.pcuk.org
The Pony Club, UK
www.shsc.org.uk
Staunton Harold Sailing Club
www.skihoo.co.uk
For Dry Ski Slope at Swadlincote
www.uk-golfguide.com

Acknowledgements

In addition to information obtained from the internet and publicity brochures, the following books were used in the research on the area.

Books:

AA, *Illustrated Guide to Britain*, Drive Publications Limited, 1985

Bell, David: *Leicestershire Ghosts & Legends*, Countryside Books, 1992

Clay, Patrick: *An Archeological Resource Assessment of the Later Bronze and Iron Age (First Millennium BC) in Leicestershire and Rutland*, University of Leicester

Coalville 150 Group: *An Account of the Whitwick Colliery Disaster 1898*, reprint 1983

Fisher, Samuel: *Reminiscences of Early Coalville*, Norwood Press, 1992

Hartley, RF: *An Archeological Resource Assessment of Post-Medieval Leicestershire*, Leicestershire Museums Service, 2000

Leicestershire Footpath Association: *Walks in Leicestershire*, Libraries and Information, 1990

Neaverson, Peter: *An Archeological Resource Assessment of Modern Leicestershire and Rutland (1750 onwards)*, University of Leicester, 2001

Peter Long (ed.): *The Hidden Places of The Heart of England*, Travel Publishing Ltd, 2000

Smith, Sheila: *A Brief History of Whitwick*, Leicestershire Libraries and Information Service, 1984

Staffordshire Federation of Women's Institutes: *The Staffordshire Village Book*, Countryside Books, Newbury, 1994

Stone, Richard: *A Srone's throw of Burton;* RSEnterprises, 2002

Swannington Heritage Trust: *Swannington Heritage Trail*

Tucker & Havers: *Mount St Bernard Abbey – The Early Years*, Mount St Bernard Abbey, 2002

ACKNOWLEDGEMENTS

Thank you to everyone who helped with this book: my family Dave, Jennifer, William and Johannes, for their support and constructive criticism; my editor and publisher for support and advice; and to all the Council, National Forest Company, other Tourist Site members and friends for their advice and contributions.

Index

A

Alrewas, 9, 86, 87, 88

Ashby Canal, 49, **55, 56**

Ashby Castle, 41, **67**, 68

Ashby de la Zouch, 14, 64, **67-68**

Ashby Woulds, 11, 12, 51, **52**, 54, 56, 63

B

Bagworth, 39, 44, **46-47**

Bailey, Hannah, 69

Bakewell, Robert, 73

Bardon Hill, 8, 18, 28, **34**, 35

Barton-under-Needwood, 9, 10, **87-89**

Barton Turns Marina, 88

Bass museum of Brewing, 81

Bass family, 81, 93

Beacon Hill, 8, 18, **22-23**

Beaumont family, 29, 32, 41

Beehive Farm, 62

Bennion, Charles, 24

Billa Barra, 35

Blackbrook Reservoir, 27

Bluebell Arboretum, 69

Bond End canal, 82

Booth, Charles, 32

Bradgate House, **25**, 30

Bradgate Park, 24-25

Braken Hurst Wood, 95

Branston Water Park, 83

Bretby, 77

Brewhouse Arts Centre, 82

Bronze age occupation, 8, 22

Broombriggs Farm, 22

Burton upon Trent, 10, 14, **81-83**

Byrkley, 93, 96

C

Cademan Wood, 33

Calke Abbey, 73, 74

Cameron, Lord, 77

Carver's Rocks, 76

Castle Gresley, 59

Catton Hall, 85

Charnwood, 13, 14, **18-35**

Church Gresley, 59

Civil war, 41, 49, 67, 68

Coalville, 44-46

Coleorton, 40-41

Conkers, 54

Cook, Thomas, 55, 67, 73

Copt Oak, 28

Coton in the Elms, 62

Countryside Commission, 4

Cropston Reservoir, 23

Croxall, 85-86

D

de Ferrers, 10-11, 24, 29, 56, 59, 63, 71, 77, 85, 94

de Holand, Robert, 74

Dimminsdale, 76

Dingle Belle, 82

Donington le Heath Manor House, 46

Donisthorpe, 56-57

Dry ski slope, 58

Duchy of Lancaster, 11, 90, 94, 95, 96

E

Early occupation, 8

East Staffordshire Flying Club, 93

Edingale, 85

Ellistown, 45

Everard, Breedon, 34

F

Fenney Windmill, 27

Ferrers Centre for Arts and Crafts, 72

Ferry bridge, 82

Foremark reservoir, 76
Foxley Wood, 61

G
Geological Landformations, 6
Gisborne, Rev. Thomas, 96
Grace Dieu Priory ruins, 29, 32-33
Grace Dieu, 32-33
Grangewood Zoo, 63
Grangewood, 63
Greaves Wood, 90, 94
Green Bank Leisure Centre, 58
Gresley, Sir Nigel, 63
Grey family, 11, 24-25, 29-30
Grey, Lady Jane, 25
Groby, 29-30

H
Harpur Crewe family, 73, 74
Hartshorne, 77
Hastings family, 11, 54, 55, 57, 59
    67, 68
Heart of the Forest, 53
Heather, 45, 47, 48
Hermitage Leisure Centre, 34
Hoar Cross, 95
Holland family, 89
Home Farm, 21
Hough Mill, 40
Huntingdon, Countess, 68

I
Ibstock, 45
Iron age occupation, 8, 22, 30, 85, 87
Ivanhoe, 41, 67, 68, 69

J
Jackson's Bank, 96
John, Duke of Bourbon, 72
Jubilee Wood, 21
Jumbricks, 48

L
Lamb, William, 72
Lancaster family, 11, 90, 94, 95, 96
Land Barons, 10, 11
Linton, 61
Litherland, Agnes, 29, 32
Lockup, 49, 69, 73
Long Close and Topwood, 61
Lount Nature Reserve, 71
Lullington, 62, 63

M
Markfield, 29
Marston's Brewery, 81
Martinshaw Wood, 30
Meadowside Leisure Centre, 83
Mease, 6, 48, 85
Medieval coalfields, 38
Melbourne, 72-73
Meynell estate, 95, 96
Millennium Chapel, 86, 87
Mining and Industries, 12
Mining techniques, 42, 50
Moira Furnace, 55
Moira, 55
Mount St Bernard Abbey, 27

N
Nanpantan Reservoir, 21
National Forest Company, 4, 15, 16, 17
National Forest Visitors Centre, 54
National Memorial Arboretum, 86, 87
Needwood Forest, 92-96
Nether Hall Wood, 77
Netherseal, 63
Newborough, 94
Newchurch, 96
Newtown Linford, 24
Normanton le Heath, 8, 48

O
Oakthorpe, 56

Old John, 24
Old Piano Workshop, 94
Outwoods, 21
Overseal, 63

P
Packington, 49
Peartree Wood, 30

R
Rangemore, 93
Ratby Burroughs, 30
Ratby, 8-9, **30**
Ravenstone, 45
Roman occupation, 8-9, 13, 23, 30, 48, 57, 63, 67, 78, 87, 89
Rosliston, 61
Royal Tigers and Centenary Wood, 47
Ryknild Street, 9, 87

S
Saint Modwen, 81
Saltersford Valley, 57
Saltways, 8, 48, 85
Sarah's Wood, 54
Scott, Sir Walter, 41, 68, 69
Sence Valley Forest Park, 47
Shirley Family, 71
Shobnall Leisure Centre, 83
Six Roads End, 90, 94
Skiing, 58
Smisby, 69
Snibston Discovery Park, 45
Springwood, 76
Stanton under Bardon, 35
Stapenhill Gardens, 83
Staunton Harold, 71, 72
Staunton Harold Reservoir, 76
Steam winding engine, 39

Stenson, William, 44
Stephenson, 14, 39, 44, 45, 46
Sullivan, Sir Arthur, 94
Swadlincote, 58-59
Swainspark, 59
Swannington, 39-40
Swarbourn river, 96
Swithland, 19, 23

T
Tame, 8, 87
Tatenhill, 93
Tatenhill Aviation, 93
Taylor family, 85
Thornton Reservoir, 35
Thringstone Fault, 7, 13, 33
Thringstone, 32-33
Ticknall, 73
Tramway bridge, 74
Trent and Mersey Canal, 87, 88
Trent Valley, 6, 8, 78, 81-89

U
Ulverscroft Priory ruins, 28, 29

W
Walton Hall, 85
Walton-on-Trent, 85
Watling Street, 8
Whitwick, 33, 34
Willesley, 57
Woodcote, 69
Woodhouse Eaves, 21
Woodville, 57
Wordsworth, William, 41
Wychnor, 88

Y
Yoxall, 96

Published by:
Landmark Publishing Ltd,
Ashbourne Hall, Cokayne Avenue, Ashbourne, Derbyshire DE6 1EJ England
e-mail: landmark@clara.net Web-site: www.landmarkpublishing.co.uk

ISBN 1 84306 106 6

© **Dean & Associates Ltd 2003**

1st edition

British Library Cataloguing in Publication Data:
A catalogue record for this book is available from the British Library

Print: Gutenberg Press Ltd, Malta

Cartography: C.M. Dean, J.M. Dean

Design: C.M. Dean

Photography: Photographs by the author

Front Cover: International memorial and Millennium Chapel for Peace and Forgiveness
at the National Memorial Arboretum, Alrewas

Back Cover: Red Deer at Calke Abbey; Walk around Thornton Reservoir